Pursuing INTIMACY *with* GOD

LIFE'S #1 PRIORITY

RANDY F. MADISON

DEDICATION

To my wife, Elizabeth, the love of my life, my soul mate
and companion. She has taught me more about
pursuing intimacy with God than anyone.
She practices what I preach.

ACKNOWLEDGMENTS

I owe the inspiration for this book to Barbara Madison, my mother, who passed away in 2009 and is now in the presence of our Lord. My mother passionately believed in me and persistently encouraged me to write some of my sermon thoughts and put them in book form. I regret that I did not do this before the Lord called her home. I hope Mom, now in the "cloud of witnesses," knows that I am carrying on in my relationship with Christ and have completed one of her homework assignments. My mother authentically modeled the pursuit of a personal, intimate, vital relationship with Christ for me and all her children. This book is all about the cultivation of that relationship. I pray that what she modeled will continue to influence others as you read the pages before you.

I also owe much thanks to the church family of the Evangelical Free Church in Hastings, Nebraska, where I have served as the Senior Pastor for the past 15 years. They have patiently listened to me, constantly encouraged and faithfully supported me. The primary basis for this book is one of my recent sermon series. The people of God at the Hastings Evangelical Free Church have tirelessly prayed for me through the years as I have sought to teach and preach the Word of God. I am grateful the Lord has allowed me to serve this wonderful body of believers.

Lastly, I thank my supportive family without whose help this book would not have been finished. I owe much to both my immediate and extended family for their encouragement and feedback. Thanks to my tireless and patient wife, children, and other extended family members the book is actually readable! May God use these chapters to "light a spark" of desire within your heart to know our Lord more deeply and intimately. If this happens, even for a few, my effort was not in vain.

CONTENTS

INTRODUCTION

T his book is about pursuing life's priorities. It is the thesis of the book that *life's first and fundamental priority* is the ardent pursuit of a personal, intimate, vital relationship with God. Often we pursue relationships, things and experiences in life that cannot satisfy the soul because the human soul was designed to find its ultimate satisfaction in the Creator not the things that He created.

Friar and author Simon Tugwell, in his book *The Beatitudes*, observed, "It is the desire for God which is the most fundamental appetite of all, and it is an appetite we can never eliminate. We may seek to disown it, but it will not go away. If we deny that it is there, we shall in fact only divert it to some other object or range of objects. And that will mean that we invest some creature or creatures with the full burden of our need for God, a burden which no creature can carry."[1] In the words of Augustine, "Thou hast created us for Thyself and our hearts are restless until they find their rest in Thee."[2] There is a God shaped vacuum in every human soul that only God can fully satisfy.

Before we begin, it is important to make perfectly clear that no one can pursue God and develop a relationship with Him *unless God has first pursued them*. We do not find God, He finds us! We do not and cannot acquire a relationship with the Creator by the magnitude of our efforts or the passion of our pursuit. The Scripture makes it clear that we do not and did not first love God. He first loved us. In 1 John 4:10, the Apostle John tells us, *"In this is love, not that we have loved God, but that He loved us and sent His Son to be the propitiation for our sins."*

The central message of the Scripture is that the fallen human race is in bondage to sin and in rebellion in our relationship with God. The history of the human experience is one of *running from God*, rather than *pursuing* a relationship with our Creator.

Romans 5:8 says, *"But God shows (demonstrates) His love for us in that while we were still sinners Christ died for us."* God's pursuit of us, by sending His Son to die for our sin, is what enables us to return to God and establish a new personal relationship with Him. It is only when we establish this new relationship by the acceptance of His free gift of salvation that we can truly begin to pursue intimacy with the One who made us.

This gift of reconciliation and salvation is given by *grace alone* and received by *faith alone* (2 Corinthians 5:17-21; Ephesians 2:8, 9). Salvation is the story of God drawing and calling us to Himself by *grace*. Sanctification is the story of God calling and drawing us into a deeper relationship with Himself *by grace*.

The pursuit of God is a life-long process enabled only by His grace. Grace is the story of God doing for us, in Christ, what we could not and cannot do for ourselves. Left to ourselves we do not and will not pursue God despite our need for Him. His prevenient grace and the operation of His Spirit bring us to Christ and open the door for the pursuit of intimacy with the One that we so desperately need. John 6:44 says, *"No one can come to me unless the Father who sent me draws him. And I will raise him up on the last day."*

Therefore, the pursuit of God is only made possible by God's pursuit of us. Pursuing intimacy with God is an enterprise undergirded by grace. It is the incredible story of the pursued becoming the pursuers of the One who loved them and died for them!

A. W. Tozer described this process of being pursued and pursuing far better than I can in the first chapter of his classic book, *The Pursuit Of God*:

Before a sinful man can think a right thought of God, there must be a work of enlightenment done within him; imperfect it may be, but a true work nonetheless, and the secret of all desiring and seeking and praying which may follow.

We pursue God because, and only because, He has first put an urge within us that spurs us to the pursuit ... it is by this prevenient drawing (John 6:44) that God takes from us every vestige of credit for the act of coming. The impulse to pursue God originates with God, but the outworking of that impulse is our following hard after Him; and all the time we are pursuing Him we are already in His hand: "Thy right hand upholdeth me."

In this divine "upholding" and human "following" there is no contradiction. All is of God, for as von Hugel teaches, God is always previous. In practice, however, (that is where God's previous work meets man's response) man must pursue God. On our part there must be positive reciprocation if this secret drawing of God is to eventuate in identifiable experience of the Divine. In the warm language of personal feeling this is stated in the Forty-second Psalm: "As the hart panteth after the waterbrooks, so panteth my soul after Thee, O God. My soul thirsteth for God, for the living God: when shall I come and appear before God?" This is deep calling unto deep, and the longing heart will understand it.[3]

C. S. Lewis aptly stated, "Creatures are not born with desires unless satisfaction for those desires exists. A baby feels hunger: well, there is such a thing as food. A duckling wants to swim: well, there is such a thing as water. If I find in myself a desire which no experience in this world can satisfy, the most probable explanation is that I was made for another world. If none of my earthly pleasures satisfy it that does not prove that the universe is a fraud. Probably, earthly pleasures were never meant to satisfy it, but only to arouse it, to suggest the real thing."[4] Lewis was speaking specifically of a longing for eternity or heaven with this thought.

However, a longing for the eternal certainly embraces a longing for the Eternal One.

Life is a made up of a series of experiences, which God often uses to wean us from our attachment to the things of this life and draw us to Himself, both before and after we come to Christ. The tools He uses; His means and methods of ridding us of the desire for things that substitute for God are as varied as the seasons of life. The journey God takes us on to rid us of our desire for other things so that we desire the One thing that truly satisfies is a life long process. It is the study of this journey and process that is the focus of the pages before you.

As you read and study the pages of this book, my prayer is, in the words of Tozer, that God by His supernatural grace, will put "an urge within you that spurs you to the pursuit" of Him. May God, by the use of these words and this study, forever change you. I pray that you will passionately desire to know Him more deeply; the One who pursued you and saved you so that you would pursue Him. *May the pursuit begin!*

> *"And you, Solomon my son, know the God of your father [have personal knowledge of Him, be acquainted with, and understand Him; appreciate, heed, and cherish Him] and serve Him with a blameless heart and a willing mind. For the Lord searches all hearts and minds and understands all the wanderings of the thoughts. If you seek Him [inquiring for and of Him and requiring Him as your first and vital necessity] you will find Him ..."* (1 Chronicles 28:9 Amplified Bible).

Chapter 1

WHAT ARE YOU PURSUING?

FIGURING OUT WHAT REALLY MATTERS!

What Rabbits Are You Chasing?

I have many memories of my time as a child growing up in Colorado Springs, Colorado. One of the things that I distinctly remember is a day at "Rocky Mountain Greyhound Park" with my grandfather. What I remember through the eyes of a child is the release of this mechanical rabbit, the sound of some bells, the opening of the gates and these greyhound dogs racing around the track at 40 mph chasing "Rocky" the rabbit.

What does greyhound dog racing have to do with pursuing priorities? Simply this: Many of us spend most of our lives running in circles at great speeds chasing rabbits. When we pause in our pursuits to analyze our behavior, it doesn't take long to realize that we humans are not much different than the greyhound dogs I observed that day as they ran at great speeds, covering about fifty-nine feet per second or 100 yards every five seconds in pursuit of that mechanical rabbit. We invest much of our time and energy pursuing "rabbits" that will not amount to much when we get to the end of our lives in light of eternity.

As you reflect on your life at the beginning of this book, two central questions may be worth asking: *(1) What rabbits are you chasing?* In other words, what are you investing your time and energy in that will not mean much when you reach the end of your life? The corollary question is equally important: *(2) What are you pursuing in your life that will last when you reach the end of the track?*

Webster describes a priority as "something meriting prior attention." A priority is something in our lives that is more important than something or someone else in our lives. A priority is something that is "prior to." In other words, "it," the priority, deserves the investment of our time, attention, and energy in advance of or before we give our time and attention to something else. Priorities identify the things in our lives that carry more "weight" and are deserving of our pursuit *before* we pursue or invest in other things.

The Bible has much to say about what is or should be most important in our lives. Many people today see the Bible as a book which is merely an ancient textbook on the subject of religion. For many in our diverse American culture, it has no relevance for modern life or daily living.

However, if a person truly values Scripture and understands the Bible, then he realizes that it is a highly relevant source book for living. In the book of Ephesians, the apostle Paul challenges us, *"Be very careful, then, how you live — not as unwise but wise, making the most of every opportunity ... ."*[1] The journey of life consists of many opportunities and the wise person chooses with discernment what possibilities to pursue in light of eternity.

The book of Proverbs, part of the "wisdom literature" in Scripture, has much to say about acquiring the commodity of wisdom as we journey through life. Wisdom is applied knowledge. To be wise is to have the ability to apply knowledge, insight, or understanding to daily life so that we make choices that lead to the pursuit of what deserves our "prior attention." When we live life with wisdom, it leads to the investment of ourselves, our time, and resources in those things that matter most.

King Solomon, the human author of much of the book, encourages us to *"Hear, my son, your father's instruction, and forsake not your mother's teaching (sources of wisdom), for they are a graceful garland for your head and pendants for your neck."* He observes, *"Wisdom cries aloud in the street, in the markets she raises her voice; at the head of the noisy streets she cries out; at the entrance of the city gates she speaks ... ."*[2]

Where Can You Turn for Help?

My wife and I are blessed to have four children, three daughters and a son. Several years ago, our second daughter, Jennifer, had the opportunity to be on the popular *The Price Is Right* game show prior to the retirement of Bob Barker. We watched with great anticipation and angst as she attempted to guess the correct prices on several items in order to move on in the game. As we agonizingly watched the video of her experience, we were tempted "to coach" her by pulling her aside, whispering our counsel in her ear, or shouting out our advice. She missed the mark with her guesses and did not move on in the game. She had to take a seat back in the audience as others got to choose door number one, two, or three.

Life's journey is often like playing *The Price Is Right*. As we move through this earthly existence each of us are presented with opportunities to make "wise guesses" on the value of a particular relationship, event, item, job, or avocation. What door should I choose? Where should "he" fit? What is more important? What should I pursue? Where should I invest my time? What deserves "prior attention"? Diogenes Laertius, a biographer of the Greek philosophers, quoted Bias, the son of Teutames: "Make wisdom your provision for the journey from youth to old age, for it is a more certain support than all other possessions."[3]

To choose wisely and pursue those priorities that are worthy of our pursuit, we often need outside help — someone whispering in our ear or shouting advice so that we get it right and choose the right door. Solomon, who wrote centuries ago, was certainly telling us this in the verses mentioned above. This is especially true when it comes to decisions involving ourselves, our perceptions, and the use of our unique abilities.

Thales, the Greek philosopher, observed that the most difficult person to know in life is yourself.[4] Recent research done by the Center For Creative Leadership — psychologists, theologians, and authors such as Richard Dunning, Thomas Merton, David Benner, and Richard Goleman — has supported this axiom and demonstrated that the feedback and advice of others is strategic in helping us to choose well and invest ourselves wisely.[5]

The Bible is our most reliable source for outside input and feedback as we journey through life. It is given to us by God, the One who created us, who wants our well-being and desires that we live a meaningful existence that brings glory to Him. It is an "outside source" of wisdom that gives us a perspective on life and understanding of what is most weighty in the eyes of God. It enables us to make good choices so that we move on through the game of life in a good way rather than being forced to take a seat in the audience. The American evangelist, Billy Graham, stated, "Knowledge is horizontal. Wisdom is vertical — it comes down from above."[6] Knowledge can be gained from personal experience, but Scripture gives us insight into that knowledge and helps us put what we learn into proper perspective.

What Should You Be Pursuing?

If one takes the time to do a brief study on the word *pursue* in the Bible, it is interesting to discover what God deems worthy of our pursuit. The word pursue is used many times in the Bible both in the Old Testament and the New Testament. The Bible is often *prescriptive* — we are commanded in various places to pursue certain things. At other times, the Scripture is *descriptive* — we are told what other people of God chose to pursue in their life.

To whet your appetite and encourage you to think and study further, I want to look at some of these representative verses and passages. Before highlighting a few of the places where the Bible uses this concept of *pursuing*, it is interesting to note what we are *not* instructed or commanded to pursue. Most of the things that we end up chasing in our lives are not on God's priority list.

For example, to my knowledge there are no references or verses where we are told to pursue wealth (the accumulation of material goods and money). I am not aware of any place where the Bible encourages the pursuit of power, fame, or success as currently defined by our culture. Most of the "stuff" on the current "Top Ten Hit List" in our modern world is not found in God's instruction and maintenance manual for our lives. Think of the hours we spend in our lifetime pursuing things that will not matter significantly at the end of this earthly life!

This introduction is designed to get *you* reflecting on *your* current priorities. What are you pursuing in your life at the present time? What is at the top of your "Top Ten List"? The purpose of this chapter is also to get you *thinking* about *some*, not all, of the things that are at the top of God's priority list. What activities does God value, in contrast to what the world around us says are important? What are we commanded to pursue?

By doing a study on selective verses that use the word "pursue," it is possible to readily identify what God considers important. Obviously, what He commands us to invest our time pursuing are priorities He considers worthy of our attention. The things on His list should be weightier than the items on our list or the agenda others may expect us to pursue.

Using the metaphor of *pursuit*, we read many times where the Bible encourages the quest of such things as healthy relationships, attributes of character (character counts in God's value system), and intimacy with our Creator and Savior: God the Father and Jesus, His Son. It is the pursuit of intimacy with God that we will zero in on in the chapters that follow.

Intimacy with God is the primary focus and singular quest of this book. However, to get you reflecting and thinking, let's look a bit further at these two other priorities on God's list before we turn our attention to the quest for a deeper relationship with the God.

God's Priority List

Healthy Relationships

"So then let us pursue what makes for peace and for mutual upbuilding" (Romans 14:19).

The Greek word used in this verse means "to pursue, to follow after, or to press forward." Here, Scripture makes it clear we are to pursue or follow after the things that make for peace in our relationships. We are told to "follow after" the things that will build up (edify — an architectural term) one another.

This verse falls at the end of a section in the book of Romans where Paul addresses people who were passing judgment on others within the church. They were causing others to take offense or stumble spiritually. Their differences of opinion centered on a person's approach to certain Jewish foods and religious days. The apostle Paul gives them a guiding principle.

To paraphrase, he is saying, "In your actions (what you do) and words (what you say) pursue what makes for peace and the building up of your brother or sister in Christ. The word for peace in this verse comes from the Hebrew word *shalom* (rest, well being, health, prosperity). It describes the pursuit of those actions and words that will lead to unity, rest, quietness, and prosperity (growth and well being) in our relationships!

"He must turn from evil and do good; he must seek peace and pursue it" (1 Peter 3:11).

This verse comes right after Peter's admonition, *"Finally, all of you, have unity of mind, sympathy, brotherly love, a tender heart, and a humble mind. Do not repay evil for evil or reviling for reviling"* (1 Peter 3:8, 9). Elizabeth and I have been married for thirty-five years. Interestingly, we are still learning to live out what these verses prescribe in our daily relationship! It is amazing how as a couple, after all of these years, we are still learning how to team together in unity, cultivate genuine sympathy (when we prefer to be selfish), and practice true tenderness rather than toughness in our relationship.

The truth is I am the one who is most frequently at fault when the wheels grind to a halt in the growth of our marriage. Far too often, I have chosen to repay evil for evil and even evil for good (when my wife intended no evil or committed none toward me). In the heat of the moment, the stress of the day, or the struggles of the work week, it is easy to slip into the mode of wanting my way rather than seeking and pursuing the building blocks that result in peace in our relationship.

Think about it! What a difference it could make in your marriage, your family, at school, on the team, in your office, at work, or in the church if we followed this one simple guideline: to pursue peace and the things that build up those around us. Our world would be a different place! Our relationships would be revolutionized! Think of the heartache that would be avoided and the heartbreak that could be stopped if this one practical principle were pursued in our routine relationships on a daily basis.

"See that no one repays anyone evil for evil, but always seek (follow after) to do good to one another and to everyone" (1 Thessalonians 5:15).

Several years ago Gene Stallings, the former head football coach of the University of Alabama, spoke at Hastings College in Hastings, Nebraska. I was interested in what Coach Stallings would share as a motivational speaker because he had led Alabama to a national championship. He also had a son born with a disability and had demonstrated incredible love and integrity in his attitude and approach to life in the midst of frequent adversity. During his speech on leadership and life, he made a pointed observation. He challenged the audience to "always do the right thing because it is the right thing to do!"

In essence, that is what Paul was challenging his readers to do in the first century A.D. in the verse of Scripture above. When we seek the good or well-being of another person we are committing ourselves to do the right thing on their behalf — for their good so that they will benefit! When we do the right thing (not the selfish thing), because it is the right thing to do no matter what we feel, then the result is peace and well-being in our relationships.

When we choose to do the "right thing," we are choosing to make a positive deposit in our relationship with another person instead of a negative withdrawal. The bank account in our relationship with that person stays full with ample cash flow and a healthy margin to protect it from going into the red.

The author of Hebrews gives us much the same command that we have seen in the previous three verses when he says, *"Strive for (pursue) peace with everyone, and for the holiness without which no one will see the Lord"* (Hebrews 12:14).

Have you ever had the experience of standing in the kitchen while casually talking with others before breakfast when you accidentally dropped a glass, and it shattered all over the floor? What did you do? Did you pretend to ignore it and nonchalantly walk into the other room insisting that someone else would clean up your mess before supper? Chances are, if you want to remain married or stay in the good grace of the rest of the family, you decided otherwise and picked up the pieces of broken glass so that no one else would step on them.

To pursue peace means that you take initiative, by the grace of God, and you make it right. When we pursue peace with others, it means we do the right thing and clean up the mess we made because it is the right thing to do. You sweep up the broken glass from the kitchen floor so that others do not get injured and a worse situation results.

> *"Turn away from evil and do good; seek peace and pursue it"* (Psalm 34:14).

This principle of pursuing peace in our relationships, as well as seeking the good of the other person, can be seen in the Old Testament also, as illustrated by this verse. Both the Hebrew and Greek words underlying this idea of "pursuit" mean to chase or pursue in a negative sense. They are often translated with the word "persecute." When you persecute someone you pursue them to do evil to them or hurt them. Instead, we are to proactively pursue people in order to edify them and bring harmony in our relationships.

When we are living in harmony, this does not mean that we agree on everything. Harmony, by definition, implies that some are singing soprano while others are singing alto; some are singing bass and others are singing the tenor part. However, the end result is a beautiful symphony of harmony to the glory of God and good of others as we journey together through life.

Godly Character

> *"Pursue love, and earnestly desire the spiritual gifts, especially that you may prophesy"* (1 Corinthians 14:1).

We often think of love as a relational dynamic, feeling, or attitude. However, love is an attribute of God that is expressed in our lives by the Spirit of God when Christ makes His home in our hearts. "Agape" describes God's love. It is an attitude we cultivate or posture we take in our relationship with others. It is an attribute of character. We are to pursue it (by and with God's grace), but the only way it will be evident (manifested) in our lives is when the Spirit of God is making His home in the center of our hearts. Christ-like character can only be produced by the Spirit of Christ.

Notice the description of the kind of love Paul is describing in 1 Corinthians 13:4-7. As you read this poetic description of love, notice that it is a portrait of the character of Christ in us — when we allow Him to have His way in our hearts and minds.

> *"Love is patient, love is kind. It does not envy, it does not boast, it is not proud. It is not rude, it is not self-seeking, it is not easily angered, it keeps no record of wrongs. Love does not delight in evil but rejoices with the truth. It always protects, always trusts, always hopes, always perseveres."*

Many modern authors, as well as ancient philosophers, have written on the importance of character, especially in the life of a leader.[7] For me, however, the thought on character that most stands out is the thought voiced by Horace Greeley when he emphasized the priority of pursuing character in the midst of all the other pursuits in life, "Fame is a vapor, popularity an accident, riches take wing. Only one thing endures — character."[8]

Notice several other verses from both the New and Old Testaments that describe the pursuit of godly character in our lives.

> *"But you, man of God, flee from all this, and pursue righteous-ness, godliness, faith, love, endurance, and gentleness"* (1 Timothy 6:11-12).

Remember how your mother would often tell you growing up, "You stay away from those boys! They are up to no good"? Other times she would warn you, "If you get near that poison ivy — run! It will make you itch!"

You were taught that there were certain things you were to *run from* and other things that you were to *run to*. In these two verses

Paul tells us what attributes of character we should pursue. In 1 Timothy 1:9-10, he tells us what we are to run from: *"People who want to get rich fall into temptation and a trap and into many foolish and harmful desires that plunge men into ruin and destruction. For the love of money is a root of all kinds of evil. Some people, eager for money, have wandered from the faith and pierced themselves with many griefs."*

We are to run from the very thing that most of this world is enamored with and chasing after! Make a special note of the fact that there is nothing inherently evil with money. It is not money but the *love of* (the endless pursuit of money) that is the root of all kinds of evil.

When having money becomes a passionate priority, it can lead us down the wrong road of chasing "rabbits" that do not matter in the end.

Before we examine the priority of pursuing a personal, vital relationship with God given to us in His instruction and maintenance manual, make a note of a few other verses that use this same biblical word and image of "pursuit" to help us identify what is truly worth chasing after in life. The cultivation of character is obviously near the top of God's "Top Ten List."

The pastoral epistles are filled with admonitions that focus on the priority of character development. Do a quick read-through of 2 Timothy, and you will discover another passage that commands us to chase after and cultivate certain character qualities that bring glory to God.

"So flee youthful passions and pursue righteousness, faith, love, and peace, along with those who call on the Lord from a pure heart" (2 Timothy 2:22-23).

Often we make the mistake of thinking that the Old Testament has very little that is relevant to our 21st century life. However, the following two verses reinforce the priority of cultivating our character above other pursuits. Proverbs 21:21 teaches us, *"Whoever pursues righteousness and kindness will find life, righteousness, and honor."* In Deuteronomy 16:20, we find this sage advice from God to the nation of Israel, *"Justice, and only justice, you shall pursue, that you may live and possess the land which the Lord your God is giving you."*

Remember Jesus' words? *"For whoever wants to save his life will lose it, but whoever loses his life for me will save it"* (Luke 9:24). Many times in life we make it our goal to inherit the land and live in it. Often, our all-consuming passion is to accumulate as much as we can and make life as comfortable as possible.

However, if we are willing to set aside our ambition(s) and make it our goal to do what is right by pursuing justice (God's will), then we end up receiving the very thing we set aside.

Our current culture puts great value on *charisma* — the personality, pathos, and ethos of a person. However, the Bible puts great value on the character of a person. You can *impress* people temporarily with charisma, but you *impact* (influence) people eternally with godly character.

In the past year, both my wife and I have lost our mothers. If you have lost someone you love, then you know what it is like to stand by their grave, reminisce, weep, and savor the memories. Standing by the grave of a loved one recently lost has a way of bringing life into perspective. It helps us clarify what is truly important in light of eternity. Going through this process enables us to identify the "Big Rocks" that we want to hold on to and not let go of. It is the process Stephen Covey called "beginning with the end in mind."[9]

If only we were wise enough to "begin with the end in mind" and keep that focus each day of our lives! Would it make a difference in what we pursue and where we invest ourselves? As we remember the legacy our mothers left us, it is not the money they made, their outward beauty, popularity, or their vivacious personalities that continue to shape and influence us.

While there was so much beautiful about them that we miss, it is the relationships they fostered and the character they forged by the enabling grace of Christ, which will direct us in our journey through life and toward heaven.

Intimacy with God

> *"Not that I have already obtained this or am already perfect, but I press on to make it my own, because Christ Jesus has made me his own. Brothers, I do not consider that I have made it my own. But one thing I do: forgetting what lies behind and straining forward to what lies ahead, I press on toward the goal for the prize of the upward call of God in Christ Jesus"* (Philippians 3:12-15).

This third and final priority is really the first and foundational priority. It is the priority of pursuing an intimate, personal relationship with the living GOD! It is this priority above all other priorities that will be the passionate focus of this book. What was Paul referring to in Philippians 3:12-15? In Philippians 3:8-10, he made it clear what his all-consuming passion and priority in life was. He was pursuing a vital, intimate, personal relationship with Jesus Christ, his Lord and Savior. Paul's passionate HEART'S DESIRE and LIFE'S PURSUIT was to KNOW HIM and BECOME LIKE HIM!

Many years ago, J. I. Packer helped my generation understand the importance of a vital, intimate, personal relationship with the living God in his classic book, *Knowing God*. In the preface to the book, he differentiated between travelers and balconeers using the imagery of John Mackay.[10] Packer's contention was that God is looking for travelers in life's journey who want to pursue an intimate, personal relationship with Him. Packer discussed the difference between knowing God and knowing *about* God when he said, "A little knowledge of God is worth more than a great deal of knowledge about Him." He went on to observe, "One can know a great deal about God without much knowledge of Him."[11]

Knowing about God but not pursuing a relationship with God seems to be the disease of so many so-called Christians in the age that we live in. The prophet Hosea issues the call to life's number one priority when he says, *"Come let us return to the LORD; for He has torn us, that He may heal us; He has struck us down, and He will bind us up ... Let us know; let us press on to know the LORD; His going out is sure as the dawn; He will come to us as the showers, as the spring rains that water the earth"* (Hosea 6:1-3).

THE ONE THING in life that will help you make sense of life is a growing, vital relationship with the Creator of life. The ULTIMATE PRIORITY that will enable you to pursue all the other important priorities is cultivating an intimate, personal relationship with the Giver of eternal life — the Lord Jesus Christ.

All things were created for Him and by Him and in Him *"all things hold together"* according to Colossians 1:16-17. He is the One who holds our lives together and brings in line all the truly important priorities in life.

Closing Challenge

I recently read the recipe offered by Tim Sanders, former chief solutions officer at Yahoo and author of *Love Is the Killer App*, for determining the priorities worth pursuing in life. He offered the following challenge in 2006. While Sanders' advice is not necessarily biblical, I still found it to be a wonderful analogy for sorting through what is truly important and what is not. Why not use this as a tool for taking inventory in your own life before moving on to Chapter Two?

Take your life and all the things that you think are important, and put them in one of three categories. These three categories are represented by three items: glass, metal, and rubber. The things that are made of rubber, when you drop them, will bounce back. Nothing really happens when these kinds of things get dropped. So, for instance (and I enjoy sporting events, so don't take me wrong here), if I miss a Seahawks' game, my life will bounce along real fine. It doesn't change anything and nothing is lost-my missing a game or a season of football will not alter my marriage or my spiritual life. I can take 'em or leave 'em. Things that are made of metal, when they get dropped, create a lot of noise. But you can recover from the drop. You miss a meeting at work, you can get the cliff notes. Or if you forget to balance your checkbook and lose track of how much you have in your account, and the bank notifies you that you have been spending more than you have-that's going to create a little bit of noise in your life, but you can recover from it. Then there are things made of glass. And when you drop one of these, it will shatter into pieces and never be the same. Even though you can piece it back together, it will still be missing some pieces. It certainly won't look the same, and I doubt that you could actually fill it up with water, because the consequences of it being broken will forever affect how it's used.[12]

If you begin with the beginning and end with the end, which is God himself, then doesn't it make sense to begin by pursing a relationship with the One who created the universe and made you? He describes himself as, *"the Alpha and Omega (A and Z), who is and who was and who is to come, the Almighty"* (Revelation 1:8).

Chapter 2

GETTING SERIOUS

A TIME FOR SOLEMNITY (JOEL 2:12-17)

John Wesley's Prayer Room

W arren Wiersbe tells the story of a sacred experience he had while pastoring Moody Church in Chicago:

> One of the most moving experiences of my life came when I stepped from John Wesley's bedroom in his London home into the little adjacent prayer room. Outside the house was the traffic noise of City Road, but inside that prayer chamber was the holy hush of God. Its only furnishings were a walnut table which holds a Greek New Testament and a candlestick, a small stool and a chair. When he was in London, Wesley entered the room early each morning to read God's Word and pray. The guide in Wesley's home told me: 'This little room was the powerhouse of Methodism!'[1]

I had a similar experience several years ago. I still remember stepping into the "holy hush" of that prayer room with my father when we were on an extended family trip to London. On the prayer table that day, to the left of the Bible there was also a piece of paper entitled "The Covenant."

At the time of our visit, the document was a standard fixture in the room along with the furnishings described by Dr. Wiersbe. I left Wesley's house that day with a copy of Wesley's Covenant Prayer which I treasure to this day. We have made the words of this prayer available to our church family on occasion at the beginning of the New Year to encourage them to go deeper in their relationship with God as they consecrate themselves to Him in a new way.

John Wesley's Covenant Prayer

I am no longer my own, but yours.
Put me to what you will,
Rank me with whom you will;
put me to doing, put me to suffering.
Let me be employed by you, or laid aside by you,
enabled for you or brought low by you.
Let me be full, let me be empty.
Let me have all things, let me have nothing.
I freely and heartily yield all things
to your pleasure and disposal.
And now, O glorious and blessed God,
Father, Son, and Holy Spirit,
you are mine, and I am yours.
So be it.
And the covenant which I have made on earth,
let it be ratified in heaven.
Amen.

Wesley often conducted covenant renewal services in Methodist assemblies in England during his life and ministry. Several times, he wrote about the spiritual results of these services in his journal. Often the services were conducted at the beginning of a new year. The words of this covenant symbolize the kind of surrender to God and intimacy with God that I am attempting to capture in this chapter and the proceeding chapters of this book as we focus on pursuing life's priorities.

Perhaps you have heard the often quoted statement by St. Augustine in his *Confessions*, "For Thou hast formed us for Thyself and our hearts are restless till they find rest in Thee."[2] If Augustine was accurate in his understanding of human nature (and I think he was), then doesn't it make perfect sense that life's first and ultimate priority be the pursuit of a relationship with the One and Only One who can bring true rest to your soul? The fundamental axiom of this book is just this!

The first priority in life should be cultivating a personal, intimate, vital relationship with God.

Are you like me? Do you ever ebb and flow in your relationship and intimacy with God (like the ocean tide coming in and going out)? Do you ever go up and down in your spiritual walk? Do you ever allow sin (wrong actions and attitudes) to creep into your heart that become a barrier in your relationship with God? Do you ever allow other things like the accumulation of stuff, the pursuit of fun, or the "busyness of business" to keep you from intimacy with God?

We are living in an age that makes the pursuit of God more difficult than it has ever been in human history. Life is moving faster than ever before. Daily, our lives are inundated with more information than we can possibly absorb, much less assimilate. The base of knowledge available to the human race on any given subject is increasing so rapidly that we lose our breath and our minds trying to keep up with everything.

The ocean of information that is one click away as we navigate the World Wide Web is endless. Modern technology which was designed to simplify and streamline our lives seems to complicate things and add to the stress of daily living. Cell phones, ipods, laptops, Facebook, twitter, mega channel choices via satellite,

Netflix, and online shopping all seem to crowd out the one pursuit worth pursuing — a relationship with God. The One Person who can bring meaning, rest and renewed purpose to our finite existence gets crowded out of our information saturated, overloaded schedules.

Taking Time Out to Get Serious!

If your heart quietly answered "yes" to any of the questions in the paragraph above, then please keep reading! We are no different, left to ourselves, apart from the grace of God, than the nation of Israel in the Old Testament. They were always ebbing and flowing, rising and falling, drifting (rebelling) and returning in their relationship with the LORD. Interestingly, the LORD knew that they would do it when He rescued them from Egypt and gave them the Promised Land (Deuteronomy 27-31, especially 31:10-13).

That is why He instituted the idea of the SOLEMN ASSEMBLY (much like Wesley's Covenant Renewal Service) in the Old Testament. Israel was supposed to observe a Solemn Assembly in the seventh month of every year on the 23rd day of the month (the eighth day of the Feast of Tabernacles or Booths) after the Day of Atonement. On that day they were to do no ordinary work but they were to assemble to remember the Lord and reconnect in their relationship with HIM. Often these Old Testament solemn assemblies were called when God's people were sinning, straying, and rebelling in their relationship with Him.

The purpose of the solemn assembly was to call them back to an intimate, personal, vital relationship with God.[3] Some of the principal assemblies recorded in Scripture took place during the reign and rule of many of Israel's great leaders like Samuel (1 Samuel 7:5-6); Solomon (2 Chronicles 7:9); Asa (2 Chronicles 15:9-15); Jehoshaphat (2 Chronicles 20:3-13); Hezekiah; Josiah; and Nehemiah (Nehemiah 8:1-8). The Hebrew word used to describe these solemn occasions describes "a day of restraint." It describes the act of holding back, refraining, or restraining from work or other things in order to focus on God.

Turning Things Around!

It is one thing to understand our need for God and another thing to solemnly and earnestly begin the pursuit of a personal, intimate, vital relationship with Him. One example of a called assembly to "turn things around" in the lives of the people in ancient Israel can be seen in Joel 2:12-17. Evidently, people were pursuing many things in their lives, and God had lost the centrality of His place within the hearts of the people. The prophet Joel was called by God to issue a spiritual wake-up call. There are several truths and principles that we can learn from a study of this situation. The prophet's call for solemnity can guide us in our own relationship with the Lord in the 21st century.

God's Call

> *"Yet even now," declares the Lord, "return to me with all your heart, with fasting, with weeping, and with mourning; and rend your hearts and not your garments." Return to the Lord, your God* (Joel 2:12-13a).

If you remember a little about the book of Joel, then you recall that Joel prophesied during a time when the spiritual tide was going out in the nation of Judah and their relationship with God. The judgment of God is imminent. He has sent a plague of locusts on the land (1:2-4) that is prophetically symbolic of a hoard of people, a powerful nation that God will bring on them as judgment if they do not change their ways (2:1-11). The Day of the Lord, a day of coming judgment, is mentioned five times (1:15; 2:1, 11, 31; 3:14) and is a dominant theme of the book.

Periodically, our nation experiences exceptionally harsh winter conditions. The months of December 2009 through February of 2010 were one of those winters that many people would like to forget! Many parts of the country were inundated with record amounts of snow and frigid weather conditions. Air traffic was grounded throughout the northeast, and travelers were stranded in Washington D.C. It reminded me of another winter season in my life. My wife and I lived in the Boston area during the winter of 1976. We experienced brutal winter conditions and record amounts of snowfall.

At the time, we were living in a summer vacation cottage with very little insulation north of Boston in the coastal community of Ipswich while I was attending Gordon-Conwell Theological Seminary. The winter winds would often blow in off the water and pound our little summer cottage. We could open the kitchen cupboards and feel the cold winter wind pouring through! Living at the end of a twenty yard driveway at the foot of an incredibly steep hill made for lots of excitement and unwanted exercise! The "winter of '76" is a winter that New England residents still remember and talk about.

The "old timers" that were living in Joel's day must have felt much the same way New Englanders do today as they recall and retell stories of the infamous winter of 1976. In Joel 1:2-3 we read these words, *"Hear this, you elders; give ear, all you inhabitants of the land! Has such a thing happened in your days or in the days of your fathers? Tell your children of it, and let your children tell their children, and their children to another generation."* They had not seen anything like this locust plague in all of their days. There had been nothing like it!

And yet God says, "EVEN NOW" — in the midst of the terrible plague that has come on them for all their sin and neglect of Him

— EVEN NOW — He gives them an opportunity to turn around and travel in a different spiritual direction.

This is the kind of God we have and worship! He is an "EVEN NOW" God! The Hebrew word "return" is repeated twice in Joel 2:12-13. The word means to turn back; to retreat; to return to the starting point. Often God will bring or allow things like snow-storms and locust plagues in our lives to get our attention and get us to turn back to HIM!

I recall another snowstorm with blizzard-like conditions that occurred in my life when we were living in Oklahoma City in the late 1980s. I was training to run my first and only marathon. I was determined to stick to my training schedule despite the severe weather that invaded our area one evening. I was about halfway through my workout when I realized that I may have made a terrible mistake. Swirling snow was accumulating rapidly on the frigid ground as the winds were gusting over forty miles per hour! By this time, I was running on a dirt road along the section line of a field. Instead of turning around, I stubbornly continued to finish my six mile run.

As I reflect on that experience, it reminds me of the way we often operate in our relationship with God. Many times we are so stubborn and sinful (determined to do it our way) that we stay the course and do not turn back. God in His severe mercy gives us another chance. He often gives us many opportunities to turn around as He did in His relationship with Israel. This is what God did in the Old Testament when the leaders of the nation called for times to "Get serious!"

In order to turn around we have to take our sin and His offer *seriously*! The word "solemn" is synonymous with the word serious. It means to be serious or to take something seriously! We live in a society where we prefer to celebrate and have fun, but there is a time in our relationship with God to reflect. There is a time to sit in silence — to be solemn and serious.

This book is best read with your Bible open and by your side. Notice the language in Joel 2 at the end of v. 12 and beginning of v. 13! There is a time for "fasting," "weeping," and mourning" about our sin and stubbornness. There is time for "rending our hearts" as we get serious, repent, and turn back to God! The word "to rend" means to cut, rip or to tear! Often we fake it at church or with God's people, and we go through the outward motions of returning to the starting point in our relationship with God — "tearing our garments." HOWEVER, God is more interested in a torn heart — a "soft" heart toward Him — than He is "spiritual" behavior that impresses others. Before we can give God "all our heart" we must have a "torn" heart (v. 12). David describes this kind of heart when he utters the following heartfelt prayer in Psalm 86:11- 12,

> *Teach me your way, O Lord, and I will walk in your truth; give me an undivided heart, that I may fear your name. I will praise you, O Lord my God, with all my heart; I will glorify your name forever* (NIV).

Here David describes a heart that is undivided and united with God! The Hebrew word for undivided or united describes the state or process of becoming one. When our hearts are "undivided" and "united" with God, then we are surrendered and intimate with God!

God's Character

> *If you choose to turn back and to seek intimacy with God, then notice the kind of God that is waiting for you! Notice the character of God. Return to the Lord, your God, for he is gracious and merciful, slow to anger, and abounding in steadfast love; and he relents over disaster. Who knows whether he will not turn and relent, and leave a blessing behind him, a grain offering and a drink offering for the Lord your God?* (Joel 2:13b, 14)

36

I vividly remember a time in my life when I was in elementary school. I do not remember the exact nature of my wrongdoing, but I do remember doing something wrong. I grew up in my early years in one of those families that operated under the unspoken household rule of, "Wait until your father gets home."

On this particular occasion, my father arrived home as he always did. However, I distinctly remember my mother mercifully pleading my case before my father. It was an intense scene, almost a struggle, as she pled for mercy and my father relented from well deserved punishment for the infraction I had committed.

This episode from my childhood is an illustration of the kind of God we have. There are many times when we blow it big time in our relationship with the Lord. God has every reason and perfect justification to punish us for what we did. CHRIST our Savior, Mediator, and Intercessor pleads our case before God the FATHER (Romans 8:34; Hebrews 2:17-18; 4:16-18). The Hebrew word "relent" used in Joel 2:14 means "to sigh, to have pity or compassion."

This is a consistent description of God's character in the Old Testament (Exodus 34:6; Nehemiah 9:16-19; Jonah 4:2; Psalm 86:15; 103:8; 145:8). God is not a God who delights in wreaking havoc and doling out disaster in our lives. He is a God who is waiting to show mercy. He is gracious and slow to anger. He is overflowing with great kindness. He wants us to know HIM in this way for who He is. The condition for experiencing God's patient forgiveness, grace, compassion, and abounding love is our willingness to RETURN TO HIM. If we will pivot and return then HE WILL RETURN TO US!

This vivid visual image of the God of creation relenting and returning is given to us many places in the Old Testament (Isaiah 30:15-18; Jeremiah 15:16-19; Hosea 6:1). The Hebrew word "to return" is used over 1,000 times in the Old Testament. In both Isaiah and Malachi, we are given the admonition to return to the Lord with the corresponding promise that He will, in turn, return to us!

Seek the Lord while he may be found; call upon him while he is near; let the wicked forsake his way, and the unrighteous man his thoughts let him return to the Lord, that He may have compassion on him, and to our God, for he will abundantly pardon (Isaiah 55:6-7).

For I the Lord do not change; therefore you, O children of Jacob, are not consumed. From the days of your fathers you have turned aside from my statutes and have not kept them. Return to me, and I will return to you, says the Lord of hosts. But you say, 'How shall we return?' (Malachi 3:6-7)

God is a God who longs to turn to us *but* He is waiting for us to return to Him! He is the kind of God who delights in "leaving a blessing for us" — providing for our every need if we will return to Him and seek Him as our first priority (Joel 2:14)!

The People's Consecration

Blow the trumpet in Zion; consecrate a fast; call a solemn assembly; gather the people. Consecrate the congregation; assemble the elders; gather the children, even nursing infants. Let the bridegroom leave his room, and the bride her chamber (Joel 2:15-16).

The Hebrew word used in this call to consecration means "to set apart; to dedicate; to proclaim or prepare." Often we have to "clear the deck" if we are serious about pursuing intimacy with God as a priority in our lives. We have to clear our lives of clutter. We have to "make time" in order to "have time" to connect with God. We have to unplug the ipod, power off the laptop, put the cell phone on silent, and turn off the television. Consecration doesn't take place accidentally, by chance. Consecration happens with intentionality, by decision, and with commitment. To make room for God means that we have to set ourselves apart for the purpose of pursuing God.

In the state of Nebraska, where I am currently serving as a pastor, football is king. When Dr. Tom Osborne retired from coaching and pursued a career in politics, the university football program experienced a gradual decline into mediocrity for several years. The excitement and synergy between the team and the fans waned.

However, under new leadership the team has rebounded and is currently back on track with its winning ways. The championship swagger has returned and the relationship between the fans and team has been renewed. The roar of the sell-out crowds at Memorial Stadium in Lincoln can be heard across the state once again. This past bowl season, the team won its bowl game in resounding fashion. However, it did not happen by accident.

They won the game impressively due to their intentionality. The coaches and team prepared diligently for the game during the month of December. The players "took a break" from normal life in order to pursue a higher goal. They were willing to lay aside their comforts and pleasures, as well as any previous achievements and rewards, in order to prepare for the game.

The Apostle Paul often used the metaphor of the athletic arena to describe his service for and relationship with Christ. In Philippians 3:7-10 he clearly tells us that he counted "everything" (all his credentials and achievements) as "loss." He considered everything as nothing — trash for the trash pile — so that he could pursue the priority of knowing Christ and becoming like Christ in his life!

Notice that this call to consecration in Joel 2:15-16 included everyone. The call issued by Joel was issued to all the people, old and young, elders and children. It even included the bridegroom and bride. In Deuteronomy 24:5, we read that it was the right and responsibility of the groom to take time away from military and public duty in order to "be happy at home" and develop a healthy relationship with his new wife. However, in this passage, even the groom and bride are called to join in consecration!

When we decide to pursue a relationship with God, it is not business as usual in our lives. It means that we are willing to give up or set aside some of the "normal" parts of our routine. Most everything in our culture, even our Christian subculture, competes with the pursuit of this priority! A.W. Tozer prophetically described our experience today over a generation ago:

> The idea of cultivation and exercise, so dear to the saints of old, has now no place in our total religious picture. It is too slow, too common. We now demand glamour and fast flowing, dramatic action. A generation of Christians reared among push buttons and automatic machines is impatient of slower and less direct methods of reaching their goals. We have been trying to apply machine-age methods to our relations with God. We read our chapter, have our short devotions and rush away, hoping to make up for our deep inward bankruptcy by attending another gospel meeting. ...The tragic results of this spirit are all about us: Shallow lives, hollow religious philosophies, the preponderance of the element of fun in gospel meetings, the glorification of men, trust in religious externalities, quasi-religious fellowships, salesmanship methods, the mistaking of dynamic personality for the power of the Spirit. These and such as these are the symptoms of an evil disease, a deep and serious malady of the soul.[4]

Tozer also stated that we are called "to an everlasting preoccupation with God."[5] God made us for a relationship with Him, and He desires for us to passionately pursue Him. As we look at the role the spiritual leaders were to play in this Solemn Assembly and the return of the people to a passionate pursuit of intimacy with God, prayerfully consider the following two questions:

(1) What is God calling you to consecrate?

(2) How does He want you to prepare?

The Priest's Contrition

Between the vestibule and the altar let the priests, the ministers of the Lord, weep and say, "Spare your people, O Lord, and make not your heritage a reproach, a byword among the nations. Why should they say among the peoples, 'Where is their God?'" (Joel 2:17).

Notice that the priests (the spiritual leaders) of the people were to set the pace in pursuing a personal relationship with God as a priority! They were to stand between the porch of the temple and altar of burnt-offering (immediately in front of the door of the Holy Place), and with weeping they were to implore God not to turn His back on His people. According to the ESV Study Bible, this was the place of prayer.[6] They were to set the pace in contrition, grieving, and repentance over sin. They were to authentically model the pursuit of God and plead for the nation of Israel before God.

Professor Emeritus Howard Hendricks from Dallas Seminary would often tell his students who were pursuing vocational ministry, "If you want your people to bleed, then you have to hemorrhage."

This thought captures what God wants from us as leaders in the church today. Elders, if you want the staff in your local church to have a passion for pursuing God, then you have to pursue intimacy with God. Staff, if you want the congregation in the church you are serving to pursue intimacy with God, then you need to pursue intimacy with God. Adult teachers and small group leaders, if you want your classes and groups to pursue intimacy with God, then you must pursue intimacy with God. Teachers and parents, if you want your children to passionately pursue God, then you will need to passionately pursue God!

41

As we close this chapter, please notice that the ultimate motivation for pursuing an intimate relationship with God is not for what we can get from God but what we can give to God — the glory of God's name (v. 17b)! The cry of the psalmist in Psalm 115:1-2 was *"Not to us, O Lord, not to us, but to your name give glory, for the sake of your steadfast love and your faithfulness! Why should the nations say, 'Where is their God?'"*

Today, God's reputation is tarnished and belittled among the nations. People see very little difference between the people of God and the peoples who do not believe in God. When the people of God passionately pursue God, then God receives the glory due to His name!

Closing Challenge

What are you pursuing with your life? What do you want out of life when you get to the end of your life? When you stand on the threshold of eternity a moment or two from now what will you wish you spent more time investing in?

Often, we can spend incredible amounts of time, energy, and focus in an effort to hit certain targets (or goals), only to discover that it was the wrong target we were aiming for. It is very possible to hit the target we are aiming for but realize later that the bull's eye we shot at was the wrong target. Matt Emmons, an Olympian, had this experience:

> Matt Emmons had the gold metal in sight. He was one shot away from claiming victory in the 2004 Olympic 50-meter-three-position rifle event. He didn't even need a bull's eye to win. His final shot merely needed to be on target. Normally, the shot he made would have received a score of 8.1, more than enough for a gold medal. But in what was described as "an extremely rare mistake in elite competition," Emmons fired at the wrong target. Standing in lane two, he fired at

the target in lane three. His score for a good shot at the wrong target? 0. Instead of a medal, Emmons ended up in eighth place. It doesn't matter how accurate you are if you are aiming at the wrong goal.[7]

God is the Beginning. God is the End. God is our Maker. God is our Savior. God is the One with whom we will spend eternity if we are in Christ. God made us for Himself. As you shoot at various targets throughout your life doesn't it make sense to make Him your primary pursuit?

Why not spend some time in your own prayer room by your own walnut table with your own Bible? Before you turn the page to the next chapter, take another look at Wesley's Covenant Prayer. Make some notes. What is God saying to you?

Chapter 3

UNLOADING OUR SIN

THE OBSTACLE
OF SIN (PSALM 51)

O n January 15, 2009, US Airways Flight 1549 took off from LaGuardia Airport in New York City. The flight was soaring smoothly in its climb through the air. However, within a matter of minutes Flight 1549 was powerless after it struck a flock of geese during takeoff. You remember the story. The ingested geese clogged and disabled both engines on the plane. The plane lost all its thrust and was in danger of spiraling to earth when Chesley Sullenberger known as Captain "Sully," a former Air Force fighter pilot, orchestrated what we now know as the "Miracle on the Hudson." He expertly assessed the situation and made the heroic decision to land the plane in the icy waters of the Hudson River rather than trying to return to the airport. His quick, wise decision saved all 155 people on board.

Many reading this story probably still have a vivid memory of that crippled plane floating in the Hudson River. As you reflect on the visual image of the crippled plane, I want you to reflect on your own life as we look at the life and experience of David in Psalm 51 in this chapter. David was climbing and soaring in his relationship with God (2 Samuel 2-10). He loved and worshipped God. He found favor with God. He was blessed by God. He enjoyed great closeness and communion in his relationship with God. Then, David committed adultery and murder, and he came crashing to earth (2 Samuel 11, 12).

Psalm 51 is the fourth and greatest of the seven penitential or confessional psalms (Psalm 6, 32, 38, 51, 102, 130, and 143). David went an entire year in denial (living in disconnect) after he coveted Bathsheba, committed adultery with her and murdered her husband, Uriah the Hittite (1 Chronicles 11:41; 2 Samuel 11). The prophet Nathan confronted him with his sin (2 Samuel 12:1-15). The result of this confrontation was David's heartfelt conviction and confession detailed in Psalm 51.

The title of Psalm 51 reads:

"To the choirmaster. A Psalm of David, when Nathan the prophet went to him, after he had gone in to Bathsheba."

Committing sin can be like flying into a flock of geese. It clogs our engines. It drains our energy. Instead of climbing and soaring it can send us into a tailspin — spiraling downward in our relationship with the Lord. In the first two chapters I have been trying to make a case for pursing a relationship with God as the first priority in our lives. The theme of this book is just this. The first priority in life is cultivating a personal, intimate, vital relationship with God. If this theme is true, then it is important to talk about sin and the effect it has on our lives and in our relationship with the Lord.

Sin disturbs and disrupts our intimate communion with God (Psalm 32:3, 4; 66:18; Proverbs 28:13). It can be a barrier to intimacy. That was the case with David. Maybe this is your situation and you are spiraling downward or you are losing thrust. You are not soaring in your pursuit of intimacy, and you know why. However, the great news is that God can rescue us from disaster and restore our intimacy with Him if we follow the Prayer of David. When he was confronted with the reality of what he had done, David came clean. He said, *"I have sinned against the LORD"* (2 Samuel 12:13). Then he penned this Psalm as a prayer and a model for us.

David's Plea of Contrition

Have mercy on me, O God, according to your steadfast love; According to your abundant mercy, blot out my transgressions. Wash me thoroughly from my iniquity, and cleanse me from my sin! (Psalm 51:1, 2)

The first thing David did once he realized he had been living in denial was to throw himself before the Lord and plead for God's grace and mercy. Now before we are too hard on David, let's admit it — we have all done what David did. We have all sinned, and often we are guilty of denying that we have done anything wrong. We deny our sin(s) like David by compartmentalizing our lives (living in one realm and thinking it does not affect the rest of my life), by stuffing the sin, by rationalizing or blaming someone (or something) else for our problem.

The church that I am currently serving hosts a "Celebrate Recovery" ministry to people who struggle with various addictions. One of the often repeated refrains we hear from the leaders of this ministry to struggling people is that everyone has "hurts, habits, and hang-ups." This is true for *everyone* regardless of our apparent level of success or status in life. We all struggle with the problem of sin, and we all tend to deny that we have a problem.

One of the absolutely hilarious videos this ministry makes available on their website is the episode of a man who is constantly followed by a pet gorilla in his life. The gorilla "appears" behind and around the gentleman in various scenes. Evidence for the presence of the gorilla is seen by discarded banana peels and other items. As you watch the video there is no denying the presence of this giant gorilla. However, the man in the video adamantly denies the obvious — having a pet gorilla!

Like David, when we truly realize we have a problem, which interrupts our intimacy with God, and we are sincerely sorry for our sin, our first response should be to plead (appeal) for God's mercy and grace. A contrite heart realizes it needs mercy, and it pleads for God's mercy. The first word for "mercy" at the beginning of verse 1 is used often in the Psalms (4:1; 6:2; 31:9; 41:4, 10:56:1, 86:3). It means to "stoop down in kindness and show favor."

The second word at the end of verse 1 describes God's tender mercy or compassion (like the womb caring for its fetus). His compassion (mercy) is abundant! God envelops us with His tender compassion when we are willing to admit the habits and hang-ups in our lives. David pleaded with the Lord, *"Have mercy on me, O God, according to your steadfast love."* The Hebrew word used here describes God's unfailing covenant love or grace in His relationship with sinful Israel. We deserve justice as we stand before God, but we can plead for mercy and grace!

David, in contrition, was pleading for God's mercy and grace on the other side of the cross. He had the Old Testament sacrificial system which was a foreshadowing of Christ's sacrifice. Jesus had not yet come and died as a perfect sacrifice for our sin. As believers, today, we have the assurance of God's abundant mercy and unending grace that covers our sin because of Christ's perfect sacrifice (Hebrews 2:17; 4:15, 16; Titus 3:4-7).

One of my favorite movies is the classic film, *Ben-Hur*, with Charlton Heston. Perhaps you remember the scene at the end of the movie when Judah Ben-Hur's mother and sister are cured of their chronic leprosy. They had been abandoned by family and friends. They were doomed to a life in the caverns and caves with other lepers for several years. At the end of the movie, when Christ dies, there is a violent thunderstorm. During the storm, streams of water run freely down Mount Calvary and Christ's blood flows mingled with the rain water. As the water carries His blood down the mountain, Ben-Hur's mother and sister, who are hiding in the crevice of a jagged rock, are dramatically cleansed and miraculously healed of their disease. The scene from this classic movie dramatically demonstrates how God's abundant mercy can wash over our sin and cleanse us like the blood of Christ mingled in the rain water flowing down from Calvary!

David's Prayer of Confession

For I know my transgressions, and my sin is ever before me. Against you, you only, have I sinned and done what is evil in your sight, so that you may be justified in your words and blameless in your judgment. Behold, I was brought forth in iniquity, and in sin did my mother conceive me. Behold, you delight in truth in the inward being, and you teach me wisdom in the secret heart (Psalm 51:3-6).

The second thing that David did as he threw himself on the mercy and grace of God (without which no sin will be forgiven) is to *openly acknowledge* his shortcomings and failure. He admitted that he sinned. He was aware that he was a sinner. David described his moral failures with three different words in Psalm 51:3-5. He used the same three words to describe his sin that he used to describe his failures before God in verses one and two.

The Hebrew word "transgressions" is descriptive of his personal rebellion. He pleads with God to "blot out" or "wipe away" his rebellious actions (v. 1). One of the greatest innovations of our time before the invention of the word processor was that little bottle of White-out that sat on your desk next to your electric typewriter. Often, when writing letters or typing documents, we make mistakes. However, because a little dab of White-out quickly covered over the mistakes we made, no error was permanent.

In Isaiah 43:25, God says, *"I, even I, am He who blots out your transgressions for my own sake, and I will not remember your sins."* In the following chapter, God speaks again, *"I have blotted out your transgressions like a cloud and your sins like a mist; return to me, for I have redeemed you"* (Isaiah 44:22). The great promise of Christianity is atonement and forgiveness of our sin because of what Christ did on the cross. As we openly acknowledge our sins and agree with God about our condition, He promises to forgive what we openly acknowledge (1 John 1:9). As we become aware of our transgressions and admit our sin before God, He is like a professor who steps to the whiteboard and wipes the slate clean. The black marks of sin are no longer visible as He erases them from His sight.

I trust that you have your Bible open in front of you as you read this chapter. Notice the second word "iniquity" in verse 5. This word is descriptive of our innate perversity or propensity to do evil. David pleads for God to *"wash me thoroughly from my iniquity"* in verse 2. The metaphor here is the analogy of dirty clothes that desperately need washing! Our sin is like a pile of dirty work clothes that need to be washed!

The final word David uses to describe his failure is the word "sin." This Hebrew term means "to miss, to trespass, to commit an offense." He repeats the word to reinforce the reality of what he has done in verses 2, 3, and 4. David begs God to *"cleanse me from my sin"* (v. 2). The idea here is an infectious (fatal) disease that needs cleansing. When we move from a state of denial to a situation of openness before and with God about our sin, we are willing to own up to what we have done and own our need for God's cleansing mercy and grace.

David uses the words "me" or "my" seven times in these verses. Is your sin a personal problem that you are willing to acknowledge before the Lord or is it a distant principle that you are aware of but not willing to own?

As David confessed his sin to the LORD, please notice that he was keenly aware of three important truths: a) Sin is *personal* — all sin is ultimately and directly against God regardless of what type and who it is against (Genesis 39:9). b) Sin is *inescapable* (apart from God's grace) — we are born with a sinful nature (Psalm 51:5).

Theologians call this the doctrine of original sin or the "depravity" of man (Job 14:4; 15:14; Ecclesiastes 7:20; Romans 5:12-14). We sin because it is our nature to sin apart from Christ. We sin because we are sinners (sinful). For many in our society, there is still a belief in the inherent moral goodness of the human race.

However, as the problems of the planet continue unabated despite the emphasis on educating people out of their ignorance, the ardent commitment to the idea that the natural propensity of people is to do the right, moral and loving thing seems to be wavering among some. Sharon Begley made the following observation in an article entitled, "The Roots of Evil" in *Newsweek* prior to The September 11 attack on America in 2001:

> In their search for the nature and roots of evil, scholars from fields as diverse as sociology, psychology, philosophy and theology are reaching a … chilling conclusion. Most people do have the capacity for horrific evil, they say: the traits of temperament and character from which evil springs are as common as flies on carrion. Psychologist Robert I. Simon, director of the program of Psychiatry and Law at Georgetown University School of Medicine, says, "The capacity for evil is a human universal."[1]

c) The third important truth that we can see from David's experience is that sin is *subtle* — it is deceptive. We are easily blindsided by it and blinded by it. We do not see it left to ourselves. Yet, God desires us to be "honest" and truthful with ourselves in the "inward being" — in the secret places of our heart. We need God's help: "Teach me wisdom (let me see your viewpoint) in the secret heart." Honesty with ourselves, God and others is the only way out of the downward spiral of sin that disrupts and destroys our relationship (intimacy) with God.

One of my favorite stories, which I read years ago and share often to illustrate God's solution to our sin, is an event that took place during the reign of Czar Nicholas II in Russia:

> When Nicholas II was Czar of Russia, a father enlisted his son in the military with the hope of instilling discipline and direction in his life. Among other things, the young man had a weakness for gambling. The atmosphere of army life seemed to hurt rather than to help him.
>
> The job he was given in the army was bookkeeping. As his gambling debts mounted, he borrowed money from the outpost treasury to cover his debts. As luck would have it, he kept losing instead of winning and sank deeper and deeper into debt. Finally, one night, contemplating his situation, he added up all his debts. When he saw the immense total, he wrote across the ledger in despair, "So great a debt, who can pay?" He then sat back in his chair, gun in hand, to reflect for a few moments. As he contemplated his life and possible suicide, he dozed off.
>
> Coincidentally, Czar Nicholas II was inspecting the outpost that particular night. When he entered the bookkeeper's shack, he saw the sleeping man, the loaded gun, and read the revealing ledger. When the young soldier awoke, he stared at the ledger and read the words, "So great a debt who can pay?" Underneath were the words, "Paid in full, Czar Nicholas II." Obviously, the Czar had the resources to pay the debt.[2]

When he died on the cross Jesus PAID IT ALL! He died for every sin you have committed (past), every sin you are committing (present) and will commit (future). If you bow before HIM as LORD and give your life to HIM as SAVIOR then His promise to you is forgiveness and cleansing of all your sin (John 3:16, 17; Romans 5:18-6:2; 2 Corinthians 5:21).

In the death of Christ, we have an infinite HEAVENLY OVER-DRAFT BANK ACCOUNT that NEVER runs out. Every time we sin and overdraw our account in our relationship with God, He supplies more money to pay our debt (by grace and in His mercy). Jesus made an account available when He died and opened it in your name when you gave your life to Him. However, it is still very important to notify the bank in order to re-establish intimacy with God.

The Apostle John emphasized the importance of keeping open channels and short accounts in our relationship with the Lord and others, "*If we say we have fellowship with him while we walk in darkness, we lie and do not practice the truth. But if we walk in the light, as he is in the light, we have fellowship with one another, and the blood of Jesus his Son cleanses us from all sin. If we say we have no sin, we deceive ourselves, and the truth is not in us. If we confess our sins, he is faithful and just to forgive us our sins and to cleanse us from all unrighteousness*" (1 John 1:6-9).

The heart of God is to cover our debt of sin and restore our relationship with the Father if we will return to Him. Jesus Christ has already paid it in full when He died on the cross. Before reading the next section, why not take a few moments to reflect on your own life? What issues or areas does God need to touch with the blood of Christ to restore intimacy with the Father?

David's Petition for Restoration

Purge me with hyssop, and I shall be clean; wash me, and I shall be whiter than snow. Let me hear joy and gladness; let the bones that you have broken rejoice. Hide your face from my sins, and blot out all my iniquities. Create in me a clean heart, O God, and renew a right spirit within me. Cast me not away from your presence, and take not your Holy Spirit from me. Restore to me the joy of your salvation, and uphold me with a willing spirit (Psalm 51:7-12).

The next thing David did as he sought to renew intimacy with God is to ask God to renew and restore him! The only way we can be made clean, new and restored is by God's grace in our lives. We cannot clean up our own act. God has to clean it up for us! We need help to become the kind of person God wants us to be! We cannot have a right attitude or the compliant spirit that wants to do God's will in our lives — God has to give it to us! We cannot restore ourselves to a personal, intimate, vital relationship with the LORD — He has to restore us! It was Augustine who said, "Free will, without God's grace and the Holy Spirit, can do nothing but sin."[3]

Notice the language in the passionate petitions of David in these verses! PURGE me (v. 7a) and WASH me (v.7b). The image here is of a leper being symbolically cleansed — by hyssop dipped into blood (Leviticus 14:6-8). In the Old Testament, the priest would take a bunch of "hyssop" and sprinkle the unclean (leprous) person with water (or blood) symbolic of ritual cleansing.[4] The prophet Isaiah recorded the heart and words of God for us, "*Come now, let us reason together, says the LORD: though your sins are like scarlet, they shall be white as snow; though they are red like crimson, they shall be as wool. If you are willing and obedient, you shall eat the good of the land*" (Isaiah 1:18, 19).

As I observed earlier, the winter of 2009 was brutal for much of our nation. Where I live in Nebraska, we went for months with snow on the ground. During periods when we received no fresh snow, the ice and snow on the ground became brown from the dirt that cars would fling onto the snow drifts as they sped down the roads and highways. However, when we would receive fresh snow, it covered the old dirty snow with a fresh cover of crystal white, fluffy flakes. The dirt on the old layers of hardened crusty ice was covered like a pristine white blanket.

This is a picture of the grace and forgiveness of God described by Isaiah. The heart of God is the restoration of our soul to pure, passionate, intimacy with Himself. However, the condition for restoration is a soft heart that responds to His voice rather than a stubborn heart that persists in sin.

Restoration to intimacy in our relationship with the Lord is a constant need and ongoing process in this earthly life. Is God moving in your heart as He did in David? Can you hear the cry of David's heart as he continues his petition? Notice the passion in his petition. CREATE in me a clean heart (v. 10a) and RENEW (rebuild or repair) a right (steadfast or faithful) spirit in me. RESTORE (return) to me the joy of your salvation (v. 12a; note v. 8) and UPHOLD (hold me up) me with a willing spirit (v. 12b)! He pleads with God not to cast him away from His presence. He begs Him not to remove His Holy Spirit from him.

This is not the time or place to discuss a comprehensive doctrine of the Holy Spirit. However, as believers, it is important to remind ourselves that we cannot lose possession of the Spirit as Old Testament believers did.[5] Having said this, it is equally important to remind ourselves that we can certainly quench the Spirit, get out of step with the Spirit and not be under the Spirit's control (Galatians 5:16-25; Ephesians 17, 18; 1 John 1:6-10).

Sometimes the LORD may "break our bones" (Psalm 51:8). He may allow us to go through pain because of our sin to bring us back to Himself and restore the joy of our salvation (Psalm 16:11; Psalm 9:14; 13:5; 35:9). God doesn't delight in breaking our bones just to cause us pain. However, the Lord is often willing to break our bones in order to break our heart and bring us back into an intimate relationship with Himself. God will break our bones in order to restore our joy.

Incidentally, "Joy is more than emotional expression; it is contented resting in God."[6] Do you remember or have you heard the familiar chorus based on this passage?

Create in me a clean heart, O God,
And renew a right spirit within me.
Create in me a clean heart, O God,

And renew a right spirit within me.
Cast me not away from Thy presence, O Lord,
And take not Thy Holy Spirit from me.
Restore unto me the joy of Thy salvation,
And renew a right spirit within me.

May God grant this kind of heart to His people in America! Oh, for more believers in the body of Christ with the heart of David! Is your inner desire to be this kind of person? Is God moving in your heart to petition Him for restoration to intimate communion with Himself? I trust you still have your Bible open beside you as you read the rest of this chapter. Notice that the result of restored intimacy and joy in our relationship with the Lord is adoration!

David's Prayer of Adoration

Then I will teach transgressors your ways, and sinners will return to you. Deliver me from blood guiltiness, O God, O God of my salvation, and my tongue will sing aloud of your righteousness. O Lord, open my lips, and my mouth will declare your praise. For you will not delight in sacrifice, or I would give it; you will not be pleased with a burnt offering. The sacrifices of God are a broken spirit; a broken and contrite heart, O God, you will not despise (Psalm 51:13-17).

David ends his psalm asking God to RESTORE HIM so that He can ADORE HIM. When our intimacy with God is restored (when we return to God), then the natural result is to reach out to others so that they, too, can (will) be restored (return to God). We want to tell others of God's saving grace and sanctifying mercy (v. 13). When intimacy with God is restored, we break out into adoration, praise and thanksgiving to God for His mercy, patience and grace in our lives (vv. 14-15)!

As you read the end of Psalm 51, notice that the key to restoring intimacy with God when that intimacy has been broken by sin is a heart that is broken and contrite. What God desires from every one of us is *"truth in the inward being"* and *"wisdom in the secret heart"* (v. 6). Here David says, *"The sacrifices of God are a broken spirit; a broken and contrite heart, O God, you will not despise"* (v. 17).

The Hebrew word broken comes from a verb that means "to burst; to break, to crush or tear." The word contrite in this verse describes a person who has been "afflicted, crushed, injured or humbled in such a way that they crumble or collapse in their heart before God." A contrite heart is another way of describing a heart that has suffered in such a way that it surrenders and yields to the Lord so that He can have His way in our lives. In another place, David gives us a glimpse of this kind of heart when he prays in Psalm 139:23-24:

Search me, O God, and know my heart!
Try me and know my thoughts!
And see if there be any grievous way in me,
And lead me in the way everlasting!

A broken spirit and a contrite heart are two keys to a heart that desires and seeks intimacy with God. God can bring good from (out of) our sin (Romans 8:28-30). When we sin, fail and realize that we are sinners and failures, then we have no place to go but back to God (through Christ). When in brokenness and contrition we turn back to God, then our sin becomes a DOORWAY to renewed intimacy and deeper fellowship with God.

Have you noticed? Often at our lowest points and weakest moments, we are closest to God if we are willing to come as David did, desiring a restored relationship and renewed intimacy. The imagery of God "dwelling" in or with the person who humbly comes to Him confessing his or her need "with a contrite and lowly spirit" is rich with comfort and consolation. The Hebrew term describes the kind of God that makes His home, actually "lodges and lies down with" those that are marked by this spirit and have this kind of heart. Is this not a description of restored intimacy with our Creator and Savior?

> *For thus says the One who is high and lifted up, who inhabits eternity, whose name is Holy: "I dwell in the high and holy place, and also with him who is of a contrite and lowly spirit, to revive the spirit of the lowly, and to revive the heart of the contrite"* (Isaiah 57:15).

Closing Challenge

The words of the Maranatha chorus are an appropriate focus and tool for prayer as we close this chapter. Why not take some time to get alone with the Lord? Ask Him to speak to your heart! Use the words of this chorus to guide you to the foot of His cross and onward to the footstool of His throne.

I Come To The Cross

I come to the cross
Seeking mercy and grace
I come to the cross
Where You died in my place

Out of my weakness
And into Your strength
Humbly I come to the cross
Your arms are open

You call me by name
You welcome this child
That was lost
You paid the price

For my guilt
And my shame
Jesus I come

Jesus I come
Jesus I come to the cross

Are YOU willing? Will you come to the cross?

> *But this is the one to whom I will look: He who is humble and contrite in spirit and trembles at my word* (Isaiah 66:2b).

Chapter 4

NOT AGAIN, LORD!

OUR STRUGGLE
WITH SUFFERING (PSALM 62)

Somewhere around 1961, almost 50 years ago, I took a trip with my dad to Denver, Colorado. We were living in Colorado Springs at the time. He took me to see a Denver Broncos football game shortly after they became a part of the old AFL (American Football League).

I still remember the trip through the eyes of a child. I can still see the playing field and the game in my mind's eye. Frank Tripucka was the quarterback for the Broncos at that time. Did you know he was the first U.S. quarterback to throw for over 3,000 yards in a season? He was also the first quarterback to throw a touchdown pass in the AFL. I do not remember who the Broncos were playing or who won the game that day.

What I do remember about the trip is staying in a Travelodge motel with Dad. I also remember visiting a large well known Assembly of God church (Calvary Temple) and hearing a sermon on Psalm 62 by Dr. Charles E. Blair, who pastored the church for over 50 years. He died in August 2009 at age 88. I remember my dad talking about the sermon.

It is this psalm, I want to consider in this chapter as we work our way through selected psalms and consider the theme of PURSUING INTIMACY WITH GOD. Are you convinced? Are you in agreement that the first priority in life is cultivating a personal, intimate, vital relationship with God?

The Tool of Suffering

Throughout our lives, God uses many means and methods to enable us to cultivate this personal relationship with Him. Suffering can be one of those means or experiences we go through that brings us to this place of intimacy with God. It can be another experience or tool that God allows or uses in our lives to enable us to develop intimacy with Him. I am not saying that this is the only reason we go through difficulty, disappointment, loss, pain, adversity or affliction. This chapter is not a comprehensive explanation for WHY we suffer. It would be foolish to make an attempt to explain or summarize all the reasons for suffering and tragedy in our lives.

Who can even pretend to have answers to overwhelming global tragedies like the devastating earthquake in Haiti in early 2010? Hundreds of thousands of lives were lost. Each of the individuals who died or suffered in that earthquake was a human being like ourselves for whom Christ died. One day life was normal and the next day life was forever changed for thousands of families and those who survived. Just this last week a young man of character, energy, personality and great promise by the name of Tobi Oyedeji was tragically killed in an early morning car accident while leaving his high school prom. How can anyone begin to explain or answer the question: Why? The tragic loss of this seventeen-year-old six foot, nine inch high school basketball star, recruited by Texas A&M University, will forever mark his family (he was their only child) and the university that embraced him by issuing him a scholarship to play at the collegiate level.

In the next few pages, we will only be looking at one small aspect of suffering. There are obviously different levels and depths of suffering. Suffering is not pleasant. Suffering is painful. We do not seek suffering. Suffering is unwanted and often avoided, at least by me! However, suffering and crisis can be a doorway, or at least an opportunity, to a deeper relationship with God, which is one of God's primary purposes for our life (John 17:3, 20-26; Phil. 3:8-10).

Many scholars believe Psalm 62 (along with Psalm 61) was written by David during a time of great pain, humiliation, suffering and loss in his life. David wrote the psalm during his exile from Jerusalem when his son Absalom conspired against him, overthrew him and David had to flee for his life (2 Samuel 15, 16). He lost his throne and power. He lost his status and reputation. You remember the story. This was the time when Shimei of the house of Saul came out and cursed David and threw rocks at him and his people (2 Samuel 16:5-7).

Think about the various sufferings in your life for a moment. What do you remember about them? Suffering often involves the *loss of something*: the loss of a loved one; the loss of health (disease or disability); the loss of a job; the loss of a relationship; the loss of a dream; the loss of freedom; the loss of recognition, reputation and position. It often leads to the loss of hope. Suffering usually involves the loss of something or someone dear to us.

David had previously lost his child (2 Samuel 12), a daughter's innocence to a brother (who committed incest with her) and his son Amnon by murder at the hands of another brother — Absalom (2 Samuel 13). He eventually lost Absalom, who sought to overthrow him. The anguish of David when he lost Absalom, his son and betrayer, is forever recorded in Scripture and resonates with all parents who have ever lost a child, *"And the king was deeply moved and went up to the chamber over the gate and wept. And as he went, he said, 'O my son Absalom, my son, my son Absalom! Would I had died instead of you, O Absalom, my son, my son!'"* (2 Samuel 18:33). If you add to this lament the years David spent running for his life and hiding in caves from Saul (1 Samuel 19-27), you realize that he was no stranger to suffering when he wrote this psalm.

Several years ago, God brought the following poem across my path, which describes the role losses can play in our pursuit of a deeper relationship with God.

Treasures

One by one God took them from me
All the things that matter most
Till I was empty handed
Every glittering toy was lost.

And I walked earth's highways
Grieving in my rags and poverty
Until I heard His voice inviting,
"Lift those empty hands to me."

And I turned my hands toward heaven
And He filled them with a store
Of His own transcendent riches
Till they could contain no more.

And at last I comprehended
With my stupid mind, and dull,
That God could not pour His riches
Into hands already full.[1]

When we experience dire distress and extreme pain, we either distance ourselves from God or draw closer to Him. As David endured the anguish of his exile and the rejection of both his son and other people, I believe he drew closer to God. He opened his empty, helpless hands to God. Notice what he says as he submits to the Lord in the midst of his suffering:

Testimony in Trial

(vv. 1-4)

His Testimony

FOR GOD ALONE (only) my soul waits in silence; FROM HIM comes my salvation. HE ONLY is my ROCK and my SALVA-TION, MY FORTRESS; I shall not be greatly shaken (v. 1-2).

Some scholars call this the "ONLY" psalm because the Hebrew particle or modifier "ONLY" (truly, alone) is repeated five times for emphasis in the first eight verses of the Psalm (vv. 1, 2, 5, 6, 7). The Christian life is one long journey in which God teaches us that our salvation comes from HIM ALONE and our ultimate security and satisfaction can be found ONLY in Him. I hope you have your Bible open as you read this chapter.

Notice the phrase *"waits in silence"* in verse one. This Hebrew word describes "stillness, quiet, speechlessness or quietly waiting." Often when we go through pain and suffering, we are dumb and numb. We are in shock and silent. We are speechless and motion-less. We do not know what to say or do. Sometimes it is like God is silent. All we can do is WAIT, endure and hang on in silence. We realize that if we are going to be delivered or saved it will come from HIM. David says salvation (deliverance, victory, welfare, health) comes from Him and is found in HIM — HE IS "my" SALVATION! Notice the word ROCK which describes a cliff, a sharp rock or boulder.

When I was a child growing up in Colorado Springs, Colorado, I remember visiting the Garden of the Gods with my parents. I was always impressed with the "Balanced Rock" in this incredible park with its variety of rock formations. If you have made the pilgrimage to this red sandstone rock garden, then you have seen this impressive rock. As a child, I always wondered how this huge boulder weighing several tons could remain sitting perfectly in the same "balanced" position on the tiny rock fulcrum or foundation upon which it rests. It sits in the same place day after day, year after year, perfectly balanced. The "Balanced Rock" is a perfect picture of the "Solid Rock," our Lord Jesus Christ. Christ is the "Rock" we can reach out for and hold on to as we go through suffering.

Notice the word FORTRESS. This Hebrew word describes a high cliff, tower or refuge. I cannot read this description without visualizing the massive Edinburgh Castle perched firmly on Castle Rock overlooking the Royal Mile that leads into the city of old Edinburgh, Scotland. Protective castles like this magnificent structure dating back to the mid-1300s can be found throughout Scotland. They are impressive physical reminders of the protective fortress the Lord desires to be in our lives when we are under the siege of suffering.

In 1 Samuel 30:1-6, we have a detailed description of severe difficulty — a season of deep disappointment and discouragement in the life of David.

Now when David and his men came to Ziklag on the third day, the Amalekites had made a raid against the Negeb and against Ziklag. They had overcome Ziklag and burned it with fire and taken captive the women and all who were in it, both small and great. They killed no one, but carried them off and went their way. And when David and his men came to the city, they found it burned with fire, and their wives and sons and daughters taken captive. Then David and the people who were with him raised their voices and wept until they had no more strength to weep. David's two wives also had been taken captive, Ahinoam of Jezreel and Abigail the widow of Nabal of Carmel. And David was greatly distressed, for the people spoke of stoning him, because all the people were bitter in soul, each for his sons and daughters. But David strengthened himself in the Lord his God.

The Hebrew word "strengthened" in verse six of this passage means "to fortify or fasten upon" — like a crab to a rock! The result is to gain strength or to be strengthened! When we fasten ourselves to God, we find strength — HIS STRENGTH — and we are not greatly SHAKEN as David testifies in Psalm 62:2. The word "shaken" means to move, slip, slide, waver or fall. We may slip, slide and lose our footing when we are hit by the winds of suffering. We may bend in the wind. We may be moved, but not removed. We may even fall, but God will not allow us to break or stay down permanently as David affirmed in Psalm 37:23-24, *"The steps of a man are established by the Lord, when He delights in his way; though he fall, he shall not be cast headlong, for the Lord upholds his hand."*

As I reflected on this theme of suffering and loss, I made a list of some of the sufferings endured by my own father over the years as he journeyed the road most of us travel from our early adult years to old age.

My Father's Sufferings
- Kidney surgery at the age of 30
- Fired — he lost his job at the age of 32
- Unsuccessful back surgery in his 40s
- Chronic back pain throughout his life
- His father died
- His mother died
- Lawsuit during the sale of his business
- Business investment disaster — he repaid the investors
- His sister (only other sibling died)
- Hepatitis B with extreme weakness and fatigue for months
- Surgery for a torn rotor cuff in his shoulder and subsequent rehab
- Heart valve surgery for mitral valve prolapse
- Pacemaker installed due to a life threatening arrhythmia
- His wife (my mother) died

As I have observed my father through each of his sufferings (losses), I have a watched a man who has (by the grace of God) *"fastened himself to God"* and gone deeper in his personal, intimate, vital relationship with God. He did not know fully what the words of this psalm meant or would mean when he and I walked out of that church building in Denver, Colorado that day in the early 1960s. However, God has *kept him,* and God has *drawn him* deeper and closer through each trial.

Each person reading this chapter has his or her own list of trials, sufferings and losses that is being written. Some reading this may even have a book filled with sufferings. You have your own "trail of tears." The journey is similar and yet different for all of us. Notice David's description of his trial as he continues in Psalm 62.

His Trial

> *How long will all of you attack a man to batter him, like a leaning wall, a tottering fence? They only plan to thrust him down from his high position. They take pleasure in falsehood. They bless with their mouths, but inwardly they curse* (v. 3, 4).

Have you ever been through an experience like this where you have been attacked or betrayed by family, friends or work associates that you trusted? Have you ever been through the pain of rejection? The hurt of rebellion? Endured the slander of your reputation? Suffered the loss of power or position?

Can't you feel David's pain as he vents his frustration, anger and feelings in these verses? When YOU have gone though suffering of whatever sort, have you ever vented like this? It is a natural human response! Part of the healing process (deliverance) is being open with our feelings and about our frustration and pain! I challenge you to do a study on the theme of suffering in the Psalter, and as you do, take special note David's openness with God!

Trust in Trouble

(vv. 5-8)

Notice that in many ways these middle verses are a repeat of the themes David gave us in his opening testimony, with a few differences. Verses 5-6 are virtually a restatement of verses 1 and 2, the refrain (main theme) of the Psalm. However, notice that here in the middle of the psalm, David introduces a few new thoughts.

Notice that it is like he is talking to himself in verses 5 through 7, and then he turns and talks to his people in verse 8. He exhorts them, coaches and encourages them to do what he is doing!

He Tells Himself

(vv. 5-7)

For God alone, O my soul, wait in silence,
for my hope is from him.
He only is my rock and my salvation,
my fortress; I shall not be shaken.
On God rests my salvation and my glory;
my mighty rock, my refuge is God.

In these three verses, David reminds or commands himself to wait in silence (be silent, rest or wait) on the Lord (v. 5a)! He reminds himself of all that God is and that he testified in the opening refrain of Psalm 62! HE is our ROCK, SALVATION and FORTRESS. HOWEVER, this time David says HE WILL NOT BE SHAKEN (v. 6b).

He adds that God is his HOPE. The term for hope used here was used to describe a cord or a rope. God is our cord of deliverance when we are in the midst of crisis. He is our rope of rescue when we are deluged with the rubble of life. He is our way out — our only way of rescue (v. 5)! David states in verse 7 that his salvation and "glory" (honor or reputation) is in God. God is the ONLY ONE who can deliver him and restore his glory or honor as king.

He reminds himself that God is his MIGHTY ROCK (the rock of his strength — a BIG BOULDER)! God is his REFUGE. The Hebrew word for refuge describes "a shelter, a place to flee for refuge or protection."

Have you ever been hiking, biking or playing golf when all of a sudden you are caught in the midst of a violent thunderstorm? I remember from my days living and vacationing in Colorado that afternoon electrical storms can roll in suddenly over the Rocky Mountains, almost without warning. During those sudden storms, it is important to find shelter for protection from the lightning and rain. Why not pause right now and take some extra time to do your own study in the book of Psalms? Notice how many times God is described in this way and with these adjectives (Psalm 18, 46, 91, and 125)! Whenever God repeats an analogy or metaphor to teach us a particular truth about Himself, it is because He wants us to remember it.

Sometimes it is necessary to talk to ourselves as well as to God. We have to tell ourselves the truth. We have to remind ourselves of what we already know. We have to give ourselves a "pep talk."

This is especially true when we are in the midst of trouble. In our pain, it is easy to forget what we already know and lose hope. We lose sight of the pavilion in the midst of the storm.

He Tells His People!

(v. 8)

Trust in him at all times, O people; pour out your heart before him; God is a refuge for us.

Here in verse 8, it is like David is giving his team a pep talk at halftime! He is no longer talking to himself, but he turns to the people around him and coaches them to do two things. His exhortation is to us, as well as the people that followed him out of Jerusalem during Absalom's rebellion.

First, he tells us we are to TRUST in the LORD *"at all times"* — not just sometimes! Are you like me? Do you ever decide when you think you can trust God and when you need to take matters into your own hands? Do you ever think or say, "Lord, I better handle this one myself?" David, like a good coach, encourages and urges us to put our confidence in Him rather than trusting in ourselves. He is a place of refuge! The Hebrew word "trust" that David uses in this verse is used 181 times in the Old Testament and 50 times in the Psalms (Note: Psalm 56:3, 4, 11; Psalm 115:9, 10, 11; Psalm 125:1; also Isaiah 26:3; 30:15)!

Second, we are to POUR OUT our heart before HIM! This Hebrew term has the sense of spilling or gushing out. There are several places in the Old Testament where the word is used (Exodus 4:9; Job 30:16; Psalm 42:4; Psalm 102 Inscription; and Psalm 142:2). I have often spent much of my time retreating within myself and stuffing my thoughts and feelings when I went through a season of suffering. With the help of others, I have been able to come to a place of vulnerability and openness with the Lord. Spilling out our heart before the Lord and pouring out our pain is the SECRET to tapping into GOD'S GRACE and gaining HIS STRENGTH as we go through suffering. There is no intimacy with another being without the pouring out of our hearts to and with that person!

I recently read a very helpful analogy in *Our Daily Bread* in a devotional by Henry Bosch. He observed, "Someone has written, suffering can lead us into one of four lands: the *barren land* in which we try to escape from it; the *broken land* in which we sink under it; the *bitter land* in which we resent it; or the *better land* in which we bear it and become a blessing to others."[2]

I have found myself in all four lands in my lifetime — the barren land of escape, the broken land of despair, the bitter land of resentment and eventually, by the grace of God and with the help of others, the better land of thanksgiving and contentment. I sincerely believe that one of the keys to the "better land" is allowing our sufferings to drive us to God and then pouring out our hearts to HIM in the midst of our pain.

Teaching on Tribulation

(v. 9-12)

In closing, David teaches us TWO fundamental TRUTHS about suffering and cultivating intimacy with God.

Truth #1: People and Power are not TRUSTWORTHY

Those of low estate are but a breath; those of high estate are a delusion; in the balances they go up; they are together lighter than a breath. Put no trust in extortion; set no vain hopes on robbery; if riches increase, set not your heart on them (v. 9-10).

Truth #2: God is TRUSTWORTHY!

Once God has spoken; twice have I heard this: that power belongs to God, and that to you, O Lord, belongs steadfast love. For you will render to a man according to his work (vv. 11-12).

In these last two verses of the "ONLY" Psalm, David teaches us three things about God that are always TRUE, which he learned through suffering.

1) God is POWERFUL (sovereign). He is the God of STRENGTH or power. The word used here is the same word as the term used in verse 7 when David describes God as our MIGHTY ROCK!

2) God is KIND. The word used here is the familiar Hebrew term *chesed*. This word, used frequently throughout the psalms and the Old Testament, describes God's loving kindness, his steadfast, unfailing, unconditional covenant love for you and me.

3) God is FAIR. He is just or righteous. These three things are true of God, even we cannot see Him or do not feel the reality of His presence in the midst of our suffering.

Closing Challenge

I am finding in my own life that suffering can be either a doorway or a wall to deeper intimacy with God, depending on how I respond to the situation. God, in His all-knowing, wise and gentle sovereignty often has allowed unwanted suffering to invade my life. It can be a doorway to deeper intimacy with God. It can become an opportunity for going deeper with God as I cultivate an intimate, vital, personal relationship with Him.

I have also allowed suffering to become a wall in my own life at times as I have struggled with the suffering God allowed to come my way. If allowed, the pain, difficulty and heartbreak God allows to touch our lives in order to bring us closer to Himself can become a barrier to the very intimacy with God that we desire and need. Where are you today? Where is your heart in this season in your life?

As we close this chapter, would you be willing to get alone with the Lord and pour out your heart to Him? Would you be willing to spill out your thoughts and feelings? Perhaps the step for you is to take time to talk to a friend, a real friend, who accepts you and is willing to understand you. Will you allow your suffering to become a doorway, or will it become a wall in your relationship with the Lord? I am reminded of the wonderful poem that has meant so much to me by Florence Willett.

Reflections

I thank God for the bitter things;
They've been a "friend to grace";
They've driven me from paths of ease
To storm the secret place.

I thank Him for the friends who failed
To fill my heart's deep need;
They've driven me to the Savior's feet,
Upon His love to feed.

I'm grateful too, through all life's way
No one could satisfy,
And so I've found in God alone
My rich, my full supply![3]

As you reflect on this poem and lift your heart to the Lord in prayer, pull out an old hymn book if you can find one. We do not use them much anymore, but they are filled with rich theology and wonderful truth. I am reminded of Augustus Toplady's hymn "Rock of Ages." It was first published in 1776. Toplady was a contemporary of John and Charles Wesley. He died at the age of 38 due to overwork, tuberculosis and frail constitution. He evidently suffered with seasons of ill health much of his life.

Thomas Hastings, a well-known American church musician who composed the familiar tune for this hymn in 1830, struggled with eye problems throughout his life. The lyrics of this hymn and its music were written by fellow sufferers who found a deeper relationship with God through their suffering. Reflect on the words as you read or sing the hymn.

Rock of Ages

Rock of Ages, cleft for me,
let me hide myself in thee;
let the water and the blood,
from thy wounded side which flowed,
be of sin the double cure;
save from wrath and make me pure.

Not the labors of my hands
can fulfill thy law's commands;
could my zeal no respite know,
could my tears forever flow,
all for sin could not atone;
thou must save, and thou alone.

Nothing in my hand I bring,
simply to the cross I cling;
naked, come to thee for dress;
helpless, look to thee for grace;
foul, I to the fountain fly;
wash me, Savior, or I die.

While I draw this fleeting breath,
when mine eyes shall close in death,
when I soar to worlds unknown,
see thee on thy judgment throne,
Rock of Ages, cleft for me,
let me hide myself in thee.

Chapter 5

Times of Darkness

OUR EXPERIENCE
WITH SADNESS (PSALM 42)

I think we all have special experiences worshipping the LORD that we remember in our lives. I can think of several, but one of mine is a memory of singing this familiar chorus "As the Deer" written by Martin Nystrom with a group of believers in Dublin, Ireland way back in 1987!

As the deer panteth for the water
So my soul longeth after you
You alone are my heart's desire
And I long to worship you
You alone are my strength, my shield
To you alone may my spirit yield
You alone are my heart's desire
And I long to worship you
You're my friend and you are my brother
Even though you are a king
And I love you more than any other
So much more than anything
I want You more than gold or silver
Only You can satisfy

You alone are the real joy giver
And the apple of my eye

It has been 22+ years since that experience in that small rented building where we were gathered that Sunday morning. However, I still remember to this day the guitars playing and the sound of that small group of believers singing as they expressed their soul's desire and thirst for a deeper relationship with God.

The day before we had been to the open market. I still remember the street evangelist and being surrounded by the massive throng of people who had no relationship with God. The chorus is rooted in, or based on, the opening two verses of Psalm 42, which we will be the focus of this chapter (along with Psalm 43) as we continue our quest for intimacy with God.

As the deer pants for streams of water, so my soul pants for you, O God. My soul thirsts for God, for the living God. When can I go and meet (appear, be near, behold the face of) with God?

Every time I hear or sing this chorus it evokes within me a thirst for a deeper personal relationship with the Living God. It calls me back to where I know I should be and need to be in my relationship with the Lord — even though I am not always there. As you begin this chapter, where are you on a scale of 1-10 in your pursuit of God? In the midst of all the other things that you are pursuing and filling your life with — where does your relationship with God rank? If we could take a "snapshot" of your life — where does He fit in the picture?

The theme of this book is very simple. The first priority in life is cultivating a personal, intimate, vital relationship with God. Someone encouraged me years ago to live my life and practice my leadership by the SIBKISS method — See It Big Keep It Simple Stupid. I have discovered that I am stupid (or stubborn) enough that I need to be reminded frequently of what is truly important or

I drift in the direction I am traveling and what I am aiming for as I live this earthly life. Pursuing a deeper relationship with the God whom we will worship and serve throughout eternity is absolutely worth pursuing; however, it is amazing how easily we lose sight of this! I recently read the following information gleaned from an article entitled, "Survey: Christians Worldwide Too Busy For God,"

> In data collected from over 20,000 Christians in 139 countries (though mostly in America) and between the ages of 15 and 88, The Obstacles to Growth Survey found that, on average, more than 4 in 10 Christians around the world say they "often" or "always" rush from task to task. About 6 in 10 Christians say that it's "often" or "always" true that "the busyness of life gets in the way of developing my relationship with God." Christians most likely to agree were from North America, Africa and Europe. While busyness afflicts both men and women, the distraction from God was more likely to affect men than women in every surveyed continent except North America, where 62 percent of women and 61 percent of men reported busyness as interfering with their relationship with God.
>
> By profession, pastors were most likely to say they rush from task to task (54 percent), which adversely affects their relationship with God (65 percent).
>
> "It's tragic and ironic: the very people who could best help us escape the bondage of busyness are themselves in chains," said Dr. Michael Zigarelli, who conducted the study at the Charleston Southern University School of Business.[1]

The message of Psalm 42 calls us back to simplicity in the midst of the stressful age that we are living in. No one knows for sure who wrote this Psalm. Some think that maybe David wrote it; however, this is unlikely. Many scholars think that it was written after the time of David by a leader of worship. It was written "TO THE CHOIRMASTER OF THE SONS OF KORAH" (note the inscription). The sons of Korah were temple musicians and singers (2 Chronicles 20:19).

This is the first psalm in Book Two of the Psalms (42-72). It is the first of seven psalms (42-49) written for the sons of Korah, this Levitical temple choir. Psalm 42 and 43 were more than likely one psalm when originally written, as can be seen from most Hebrew manuscripts. There is a common refrain or theme that ties these psalms together (42:5, 42:11; 43:5).

Why are you cast down, O my soul,
and why are you in turmoil within me?
Hope in God; for I shall again praise him,
my salvation and my God.

Desire in Distress

Psalm 42:1-5

What we do know is that whoever wrote the psalm is in exile. He is a long way from the temple in Jerusalem. He is being taunted, ridiculed or mocked by those who do not believe in God (v. 3b). He is distressed and disheartened, discouraged or despondent (v. 3a, 5). He is disconnected from the temple (the place of worship). His tears are his food day and night as he reminisces and remembers the "good old days" when he used to lead the procession in worship to the *"house of God"* (v. 4).

The two things that stand out to me in this opening stanza are the DESIRE and the DISTRESS of the writer. He has this DEEP YEARNING or ARDENT DESIRE to be back in Jerusalem and reunited with God's people processing to the temple *"with glad shouts and songs of praise," "a multitude keeping festival"* (v. 4). He is feeding on his tears and longing like a hunted deer for water to connect in worship with God. We all have images from the movies or personal experience of a panting deer running for her life as she is being chased by hunters. The frantic doe pauses momentarily, panting as it longingly looks for water that will renew and refresh as she runs for her life.

I still remember one of the first Nebraska football games I went to at Memorial Stadium in Lincoln soon after we moved to the "Big Red" state. It was an incredibly beautiful fall day, and excitement was at a fever pitch. We have all had the experience of "game day" and the anticipation that is a part of that experience during football season. Would you equate your excitement and desire for intimacy with God to your excitement and desire to be in your favorite football stadium on game day? Would you compare it to the thirst (panting) of a hunted deer for water? When was the last time you cried for days because you longed to behold the face of God and be in intimate communion with Him? The Hebrew word "Elohim," which describes the sovereign, triune God, is repeated sixteen times in Psalms 42-43 and 188 times in Book Two of the Psalter.

I am reminded of a brief snapshot of the beginning of the historic Welsh Revival that began in 1904 and spread throughout the world.

> A century ago Wales experienced the last National Religious Revival, a revival that brought in an extra 100,000 new converts according to the estimates of the time, and a movement that quickly spread to the four corners of the World. Yet that great move of the Spirit had *very small beginnings*. Beginnings that didn't always involve the great preachers of the day-erudite and educated as they were, but instead included, for instance, a young teenager from New Quay, Cardigan, Florrie Evans, who in a youth meeting in February 1904 declared publicly that she *loved the Lord Jesus with all her heart*. With these words the Spirit seemed to fall on the meeting and the fire quickly spread to other young people in the Cardiganshire area.

After the first stirrings amongst the young women of New Quay, young women continued to play a part in the Revival work — young Florrie went on a team to North Wales with her friend Maud — others used their voices as instruments of God's message. People were changed in so many ways. The crime rate dropped, drunkards were reformed, pubs reported losses in trade. Even football and rugby became uninteresting in the light of new joy and direction received by the converts. The public excitement of the Revival had died down by 1906. The newspapers went back to politics and other things, but for many, the honeymoon of these 2 years developed into a lasting and loving relationship with a risen Christ that continued a lifetime.

In asking one elderly Revival convert some years ago as to whether the Revival stopped in 1906, she answered — it's still burning within my heart — it's never been extinguished — it had burned for over 70 years.[2]

When we reach the place in our hearts of that young Florrie Evans who said, "Oh, how I love Jesus" and people hear and see this kind of longing for the Lord, then maybe the revival that many in our nation have been praying for will begin!

Times of Darkness Can Be a Doorway

Many times God will use times of darkness or depression to usher in new seasons of light and exaltation in our relationship with God. Often the precursor to revival in our own hearts and a renewed desire for a deeper relationship with God is preceded by a season of despondency. Notice in Psalm 42 that the person writing these words is DISTRESSED! He is disheartened (heartsick) and discouraged. He is sad and crying. He is down in the dumps.

Why are you cast down, O my soul,
and why are you in turmoil within me?

Hope in God; for I shall again praise him,
my salvation.

The word the psalmist uses to describe the condition of his soul, *"cast down,"* describes being in the pit, sinking down or being depressed. It is the same word that David uses to describe the state of his soul and stirring for the Lord that results in Psalm 38:6-9, *"I am utterly bowed down and prostrate; all the day I go about mourning. For my sides are filled with burning, and there is no soundness in my flesh. I am feeble and crushed; I groan because of the tumult of my heart. O Lord, all my longing is before you; my sighing is not hidden from you."*
The word "tumult" or turmoil describes "commotion or an uproar." It means to be "disturbed," "disquieted," or agitated — all stirred up. I do not know where you are in your own life at the present time. However, you may be in the same emotional condition this man was when he wrote this psalm. These words describe the state of your soul and sigh of your inner being. You may be distressed and disheartened. Your circumstances are obviously different than the person who penned these words — you are not in exile, and you are not being belittled for your belief in the same way he was.
However, when we are distressed and disheartened, it is usually because of some circumstance in our lives that is going south, in a direction we do not want. Can you identify with the psalmist?
The point I want you to see is that God can use distressing, even disheartening, circumstances which we do not want and would not choose to bring us back to where we would not go in our relationship with Him. Unwanted circumstances can be a doorway to a deeper relationship with the Lord if we are open to learning from them.
Notice the way out of distress and despondency is to "HOPE" (wait on, trust) in God who is our SALVATION (v. 5b; 11b; 43:5b)! Waiting *on* God and *for* God is often a process. Waiting on God to

deliver us and bring us back into a right relationship with Himself is not pleasant. Waiting on God is difficult, if not impossible, in our culture of instant gratification, where the expectation is often for an immediate solution to our situation. The word "process" is a term that could almost be dropped from the English language. However, often what we learn in the process of coming back into renewed relationship with the Lord is as valuable and important as the product, the end result.

Dialogue in Depression

Psalm 42:6-11

In the second stanza of the psalm we have a picture of the psalmist's dialogue in the midst of his depression. Look at verse 6 and then study verse 11! This second stanza opens with the writer saying, *"My soul is cast down within me,"* and he ends Psalm 42 by repeating the refrain again, *"Why are you cast down, O my soul, and why are you in turmoil within me?"*

The writer is not only disheartened, he is depressed! He is in the pit! Notice what he says in verse 7, *"Deep calls to deep at the roar of your waterfalls; all your breakers and your waves have gone over me."* HAVE YOU EVER FELT LIKE THIS?

I distinctly remember a New Year's day spent lying on the living room floor in our home while we were living in Oklahoma City, Oklahoma. I spent several hours, as I recall, reading, praying and journaling. You know the kind of morning it was. We have all had those seasons and experiences. My hair was disheveled and my breath was bad. I was down emotionally, tired physically and washed out mentally. I was trying to make sense of my circumstances and felt like I was at a crossroad in my life vocationally. I was earnestly seeking the Lord and His guidance in the midst of unwelcomed events that I had not anticipated and did not understand.

As I read verse 7 of this psalm that particular morning, I readily identified with the graphic description of the writer and thought, "YES, LORD, 'all your breakers and your waves have gone over me.'" I was tired, down and depressed. Little did I know that all His waves and breakers had not gone over me! There were still many more breakers and waves to come!

That is the way life is. It is often composed of a series of events and experiences that God orchestrates and allows to come our direction. He often uses life's waves to wash us to shore and bring us back to Himself. This was Jonah's experience. In Jonah 2:3 we read, *"For you cast me into the deep, into the heart of the seas, and the flood surrounded me; all your waves and billows passed over me."*

When Jonah cried out to the Lord in his distress, from the belly of the fish, and confessed the things that were keeping him from a deeper, more compliant relationship with God, then the Lord released him from the belly of the fish. Jonah observed, *"Those who cling to worthless idols forfeit the grace that could be theirs."*[3] The Lord led Jonah through his distress and depression into His grace and on to terra firma — dry ground!

Throughout my life, I have struggled with both anxiety and depression. Neither are emotional experiences I prefer to go through. None of us want to be depressed or go through turmoil. Yet, when God allows these emotions and experiences to come our way, they can be tools that make us take a look at life from another perspective — God's perspective.

When we begin to reflect and lift our hearts to the Lord, as Jonah did and as the psalmist does in Psalm 42, then our heartfelt cries to God become a road out of the distress and into intimacy with Lord. In the end, as we observed in the last chapter on suffering, depressing emotions and experiences (sad times) can be a road back to intimacy with God and greater dependence on Him!

The purpose of this chapter is not to explain circumstantial or systemic depression. It is not a discussion about the comprehensive causes and cures of depression. For those struggling with chronic anxiety or deep depression which doesn't decrease in intensity, please note a few resources given at the end of the book.[4] However, I hope you realize now that if you are struggling with some form of depression in your life, then you are not alone! If you feel like you are in "exile" like the psalmist, then you are in good company. Many people whom God has used to accomplish His purposes throughout church history and in modern times have struggled with depression.

William Cowper, the great 18th century hymnist, battled chronic depression and times of deep emotional darkness. One foggy night in London, England, he hit what he thought was absolute bottom and attempted suicide in 1772. He actually attempted suicide several times during his life and ministry.[5] John Bunyan, author of *The Pilgrim's Progress* and *Grace Abounding* struggled greatly with obsessive compulsive disorder and the despondency that goes along with the disease.[6] Kent Hughes describes and details the struggles with depression of well known Christian leaders and pastors such as, C. H. Spurgeon, John Henry Jowett, Alexander Whyte and Martin Luther in his book, *The Success Syndrome*.[7]

If you are vulnerable to times of despondency like I am, then you may find comfort in one episode from the life of Spurgeon. "On an unforgettable Sunday morning in 1866, the great C. H. Spurgeon stunned his five thousand listeners when from the pulpit of London's Metropolitan Tabernacle he announced, "I am the subject of depressions of spirit so fearful that I hope none of you ever gets to such extremes of wretchedness as I go to."[8] John Piper, one of Spurgeon's 21st century admirers, observed that Spurgeon "viewed his depression as a part of God's plan. His unwavering confidence in divine sovereignty kept him from caving in. He could see that God was using his struggles to keep him humble, to pour out more power through his ministry, and to prepare him for greater usefulness."[9] Joanie Yoder, author and contributor to the devotional *Our Daily Bread*, discussed openly her struggle with anxiety before she went home to be with the Lord in 2004 and wrote two helpful books.[10] Beth Moore, renowned speaker and author, has also discussed her own struggle with depression.[11]

Psychologist Arthur E. Jongsma, Jr. writes, "Depression is not just a brief feeling of unhappiness or disappointment with the circumstances of life ... It is a pervasive, crippling, extended feeling of helplessness and hopelessness."[12] The man who wrote Psalm 42 was, I believe, struggling with "an extended feeling of helplessness and hopelessness." He has been in the malaise of despondency for some time and is wondering when God will restore his sense of inner joy and peace as he reaches out to Him. Notice that he does three things that can be helpful to all of as we dig ourselves out of the pit of despair that invades our lives from time to time.

He Remembers God's Fellowship

(v. 6)

He reminds himself of the Lord and times of sweet communion with Him on Mount Mizar (location unknown). This can be an anchor to our soul and keep us focused on the truth. Our view of reality can be skewed when we are despairing. Things often look worse than they really are. It is important to remind ourselves of better times when our communion with God was sweet. Spurgeon comments, "He recalls his seasons of choice communion by the river and among the hills, and especially that dearest hour upon the little hill, where love spake her sweetest language and revealed her nearest fellowship. It is great wisdom to store up in memory our choice occasions of converse with heaven, we may want them another day ..."[13]

He Reminds Himself of God's Presence

(v. 8, 9)

Notice that he remembers a) God's steadfast *love* that is with him during the day (v. 8) b) God's *song* that is with him at night (v. 8) and c) God's *strength* that holds him up (v. 9). He opens verse 9 with a statement, and then he asks a question, *"I say to God my rock: Why have you forgotten me?"* The word translated "rock" describes a fortress, or stronghold (Psalm 18:2; 40:2). This descriptor of Elohim is used 55 times in th Old Testament and 9 times in the book of Psalms.

The LORD is with him 24/7, whether he sees it or not. When we are depressed and in despair, we do not see life as it really is. God's steadfast love, song, and strength are three unchanging realities, which are unequivocally and eternally true, regardless of our circumstances or how we may feel at any given moment. These eternal truths are *anchors* for our soul.

He Reflects on His Emotions

(v. 9, 11)

Notice that he asks why! He asks the "WHY" question ten times in this psalm! He asks it four times in these two verses! This is a recommended recipe for good emotional and mental health! It is a natural human response when we are down in the dumps.

I had a Christian counselor tell me during one counseling session to "lift up the hood" on my "emotional" automobile and check underneath to see what is causing the "smoke" when I am in emotional turmoil, anxious or depressed. The worst thing we can do when we go through times of despair is to STUFF IT and pretend that every thing is OK.

Notice that the psalmist dialogues with himself, and he talks to God. He is OPEN about what he feels and what he perceives in verse 9 — *"Why have you forgotten me?"* Often life feels this way when we are down. We feel like God has abandoned us and we are all alone. C. H. Spurgeon, no stranger to the pond of despair, recommended honesty with God and oneself as spiritual therapy for the down times we experience. He commented, "As Trapp says, 'David chideth David out of the dumps;' and herein he is an example for all desponding ones. To search out the cause of our sorrow is often the best surgery for grief. Self-ignorance is not bliss; in this case it is misery. The mist of ignorance magnifies the causes of our alarm; a clearer view will make monsters dwindle into trifles."[14]

Deliverance in Despair

Psalm 43:1-5

Psalm 43 is a continuation of all of the themes in Psalm 42 and concludes with the same refrain in verse 5! One commentator interpreted these psalms in this way, "In stanza one, we see faith's rebuke to dejection (42:5). In stanza two, we see faith's encouragement in confusion (42:11). In stanza three, we see faith's triumphant declaration of certainty (43:5)."[15]

We have a perfect picture of a person who is distressed, depressed and in despair who digs himself out of the pit by the enabling grace of God and enters into a deeper relationship with God because of what he endures. Notice the tone of victory and restored intimacy with the Lord in Psalm 43:1-4!

Vindicate me, O God, and defend my cause against an ungodly people, from the deceitful and unjust man deliver me! For you are the God in whom I take refuge; why have you rejected me? Why do I go about mourning because of the oppression of the enemy?

Send out your light and your truth; let them lead me; let them bring me to your holy hill and to your dwelling (tent; tabernacle)! Then I will go to the altar of God, to God my exceeding joy, and I will praise you with the lyre, O God, my God. (v. 1-4)

As a young pastor, I read the following story in one of the many books that I utilize for sermon preparation. The story serves as a grim reminder of the reality that things are not always on the inside as they appear on the outside to other people.

"I Am Grimaldi"

One evening in 1808, a gaunt, sad-faced man entered the office of Dr. James Hamilton in Manchester, England. The doctor was struck by the melancholic appearance of his visitor. He inquired: "Are you sick?"

"Yes, doctor, sick of a mortal malady."
"What malady?"

"I am frightened of the terror of the world around me. I am depressed by life. I can find no happiness anywhere, nothing amuses me, I have nothing to live for. If you cannot help me, I shall kill myself."

"The malady is not mortal. You only need to get out of yourself. You need to laugh; to get some pleasure from life."

"What shall I do?"

"Go to the circus tonight to see Grimaldi, the clown. Grimaldi is the funniest man alive. He will cure you."

A spasm of pain crossed the poor man's face as he said: *"Doctor, don't jest with me; I am Grimaldi."*[16]

When you find yourself in the pond of despair, get the help that you need. At times, medication and therapy or counseling may be needed. God has provided many good resources to help us climb out of the pit. However, as you make the climb, keep your heart open to the Lord and the lessons He may be trying to teach you. Sadness, like suffering, is another one of those experiences God allows to come our way to draw us into a more intimate, vital relationship with Him. Ultimately, the way out of the pit of despair is a deeper relationship with God. He is the only one who can satisfy the deepest desires of our soul.

> *"Why are you cast down, O my soul, and why are you in turmoil within me? HOPE IN GOD; FOR I SHALL AGAIN PRAISE HIM, MY SALVATION AND MY GOD* (Psalm 43:5).

Closing Challenge

Consider the following poem:

Feeling blue?
Buy some clothes.
Feeling lonely?
Turn on the radio.

Feeling despondent?
Read a funny book.
Feeling bored?
Watch TV.

Feeling empty?
Eat a sundae.
Feeling worthless?
Clean the house.

Feeling sad?
Tell a joke.
Ain't this modern age wonderful?
You don't gotta feel nothin',

There's a substitute for everythin'!
God have mercy on us![17]

Reflect on this poem; ask yourself the hard questions. Take time for some inventory of the soul. What are you currently filling your life with to dull the pain of depression, boredom, emptiness or sadness? Does God want to use your situation to teach you more about Him? Are you willing to seek satisfaction in the Savior?

Chapter 6

DRY TIMES MAKE ME THIRSTY

OUR ENCOUNTER
WITH SAHARA (PSALM 63)

Webster's New Collegiate Dictionary defines a "desert" as "an arid, barren stretch of land incapable of supporting any considerable population without an artificial water supply; a desolate or forbidding place."

There are many famous deserts. One example is the Mojave Desert in the southwestern United States where temperatures get as high as 120-130 degrees F. It receives less than 10 inches of rain a year. The Great Sandy Desert in Australia is about the size of Japan. The Peruvian Desert in South America is another intimidating piece of real estate.

The largest desert in the world is the Sahara Desert. It is 3.5 million square miles and covers most of Northern Africa. It is almost as big as the United States or the continent of Europe. It receives less than 3 inches of rain a year and temperatures get as high as 136 degrees F! You don't want to get lost in the Sahara Desert!

Most of us prefer to avoid the desert. Deserts and desert experiences can be painful and life threatening. However, God can use desert experiences to create in us a thirst for the only One who can quench that thirst. Often, desert experiences can be times that God allows to draw us back to Him, the Giver of living water.

As you work your way through this chapter and look at a desert experience in the life of David, you will once again need your Bible. Psalm 63 is the text we will consider as we continue this study on pursuing intimacy with God. When David wrote this psalm, he was "wandering in the wilderness" of Judah. David most likely wrote this psalm when he was in exile during Absalom's rebellion. He wrote it along with Psalm 62 when he was wandering in exile, banished from Jerusalem in the desert.

The wilderness, or desert of Judah, is 19 miles southwest of Jerusalem. In Bible times, the desert of Judah was a place of refuge for those who were wandering or in exile from enemies. David spent a lot of time in the wilderness of Judah in his early years when he was running from King Saul.

I don't know what comes to your mind when I say the word "desert," but the two images that come to my mind are the image of someplace very *dry* and the idea of *thirst* — a place where there is no water. That was David's experience as he wrote this psalm. It was dry. He describes his experience in the very first verse of the psalm as he remembers his time in the wilderness of Judah and the effect it had on his relationship with God. *"My soul thirsts for you; my flesh faints for you, as in a dry and weary land where there is no water."*

David was tired as he trudged through the desert (2 Samuel 16:2, 14; 17:29; Psalm 63:1). He was struggling and suffering (2 Samuel 15-16). He walked barefoot and with his head covered as he left the capitol city of Jerusalem (2 Samuel 15:30). It was all he could do to put one foot in front of the other. He was hungry and thirsty (2 Samuel 17:29).

If you have lived long enough, then chances are you have had some sort of "desert experience" in your own spiritual journey and walk with the Lord. If you have, then I want to encourage you.

Sahara times, like sad times and seasons of suffering, can be another tool or means God uses to bring us back into a deeper more intimate relationship with HIM. God is relentless in His love. He is ruthless in His pursuit of us because He wants us to realize that the first priority in life is cultivating a personal, intimate, vital relationship with God.

There are three questions I want to ask and attempt to answer in the remainder of this chapter: 1) What does the desert look like? 2) How do we get into the desert? 3) What are the effects of the desert?

#1 — What Does the Desert Look Like?

Desert experiences can be different for all of us. They are hard to describe and difficult to define or get a handle on. Many times, when we first enter the desert we do not even realize that we are there — *in the desert*. It is only after we have been there for a while trying to find our way out that we realize we allowed ourselves to stumble into the spiritual wilderness. However, if you are in a desert time — a dry time in your relationship with God — then chances are you feel a) isolated b) miserable and c) distant from God. I am sure there are many other characteristics or marks of a desert experience or season, but I am convinced that one of the marks is that we often feel "deserted" while we are in the desert.

Isolation

Usually when you hear about someone who is lost or dies in the desert, they are alone (or with a few other people). You do not usually get lost or die in the desert with a large group of people. If you were in a big group, you probably never would be there in the first place!

Later in this chapter, I will talk about one of my "desert" experiences. One of the things that I distinctly remember was feeling isolated, alone, with no real friends. I believe David felt this way as he left Jerusalem during Absalom's rebellion. Read the story in 2 Samuel 15-17. He felt alone — disconnected (even though he was surrounded by many people who were loyal to him).

Have you ever had the experience of going through a dry season spiritually? Often, you can find yourself in a room surrounded by people, however, you feel like you are alone — the only one in the room.

Miserable

When you are in the desert you can feel MISERABLE. It is a time of suffering. It is hot and dry. You are thirsty (emotionally and spiritually) for something else or something more in your relationship with God and others. You are tired, cold and hungry (physically and emotionally). When you go through a desert experience, you feel all the things that happen to people when they are stuck in the desert. A person can get discouraged, lose hope and want to quit in the middle of the desert. Read David's story in 2 Samuel 15 through 17 and see how many of these characteristics, feelings, or emotions you can find in his life.

Distance

During spiritual and emotional dry times, you can experience a DISTANCE between yourself and the Lord. It is like you are out there in the Sahara, you are all alone, you are crying for help and there is no answer. God seems distant and unresponsive even though you are crying for deliverance or desperately looking for a way out. I think David felt abandoned by the Lord or at least wondered where He was many times in his life — read the psalms.

Recall the experience of the psalmist in Psalm 42 in the previous chapter. Reflect on the words of Asaph in Psalm 77:7-9, as he endured his own desert time, "Will the Lord spurn forever, and never again be favorable? Has His steadfast love forever ceased? Are His promises at an end for all time? Has God forgotten to be gracious? Has He in anger shut up His compassion?"

#2 — How Do We Get Into the Desert?

I do not know anybody that wakes up one morning and says to himself or herself, "You know, life is going really well right now. I think I will mess it up and see if I can't feel isolated, miserable and distant from God! However, I think there are many reasons why we can go through desert times. There are many roads into the desert.

Simple Stupidity

Sometimes we end up in the desert in our lives out of simple stupidity. We make a bad or wrong decision unintentionally or unknowingly. That was not the case with David. He ends up in the wilderness of Judah for other reasons.

However, mistakes in judgment, failure to listen to the wise counsel of others or hasty decisions without getting all of the facts can lead us into painful situations that result in desert-like conditions in our lives. In Proverbs 24:6-7 we find this reminder and caution, *"For by wise guidance you can wage war, and in abundance of counselors there is victory. Wisdom is too high for a fool; in the gate he does not open his mouth."* The city gate in ancient Israel was a place where the city elders would gather and young men could glean wisdom from their experience.

Proverbs 19:2-3 says, *"Desire without knowledge is not good, and whoever makes haste with his feet misses his way. When a man's folly brings his way to ruin, his heart rages against the Lord."* A similar thought is etched on the pages of Scripture in Proverbs 21:5, *"The plans of the diligent lead surely to abundance, but everyone who is hasty comes to poverty."* Each of these verses stands like the yellow flashing light at a busy intersection. They shout their message, "Proceed with caution!" They are God's warnings to tell you that if not followed, a dry time in the desert is just around the corner.

The following case study titled "Lost in the Desert" is a true story about a man named Mark who ended up lost in the Mojave Desert. It illustrates how easily and almost effortlessly we can end up stranded in the wilderness without meaning to.

Mark, a white, 35-year-old male weighing approximately 70 kilograms, started a three-hour drive across the desert on U.S. 95 from Yuma, Arizona, to Blythe, California. He set out at 7:00 a.m. on what was expected to be a very hot July day. He anticipated that it would take him about three hours to reach Blythe — plenty of time to make his 11:00 a.m. appointment with Sarah, his fiancée. When he failed to appear by noon, Sarah became concerned and called the highway patrol.

By 12:20 p.m, Search and Rescue officer Maria Arroyo reported an abandoned car on the side of the road with a damaged radiator that matched Sarah's description of Mark's vehicle. The officer noticed shoe prints leading into the desert toward some low mountains in the distance. Maria called for helicopter assistance, consulted her GPS, and relayed the exact coordinates to base.

By 1:00 p.m. Henry Morningstar, paramedic and a member of the helicopter crew, reported a shirtless, hatless man wandering down a desert wash. The air temperature was hovering around 105 degrees Fahrenheit in the shade (and there was darn little of that). The relative humidity was less than 5 percent. The helicopter crew members spotted a man staggering on the desert. They realized they had found

Mark. His driver's license identified him as the missing man. Mark was still conscious, but clearly delirious. He was weak, nauseous, disoriented and complained of a headache. His blood pressure was low-70/50 and he was not sweating despite oppressive heat. His body temperature was 105 degrees. He was diagnosed with heat stroke and first degree burns on his face and back.

Fortunately, Mark was rescued in time to spare his life and enable his recovery. As he recovered in the hospital, he related what happened to him earlier in the day. Since he was a newcomer to desert areas, he *saw no need to bring UV A/B sunblock or extra water* on his trip from Yuma to Blythe. He recalled seeing a coyote dart out between two bushes, and he seemed to recollect hitting the animal. The area was so isolated that his cell phone was useless. He waited by the car for a while, but then about 10:00 a.m., as the sun climbed, *he saw a large body of water in the distance, possibly, he thought, the Colorado River.* The "river" was in reality, a mirage, as he realized later after he had walked some distance. He then became confused and could not find his way back to the highway.[1]

Sometimes we unintentionally stumble into seasons of spiritual dryness. We fail to follow God's wisdom and warning signs, so we find ourselves wandering in the wilderness. However, there are other times when we experience spiritual dryness, and it is because we willfully pursue a certain path that leads us into the desert. We bring the desert experience on ourselves.

Sinful Stubbornness

There are times in our lives when we can end up in a desert situation or experience due to our sinful disobedience. In other words, we know what God wants us to do, but in our own human stubbornness we persist in traveling in a certain direction, so we end up

99

in the desert! God will allow us to take the road we want because He desires for us to follow Him willingly — out of love, not coercion. We think we know better than God does, and we end up on the back side of the desert, in the SAHARA.

This was certainly the case with David. The reason for his desert experience can be traced back to his sin with Bathsheba and the murder of Uriah the Hittite (2 Samuel 11, 12:9-15). I believe Psalm 106:13-15 in the King James Version describes this kind of situation, *"They soon forgot his works; they waited not for his counsel: But lusted exceedingly in the wilderness, and tempted God in the desert. And he gave them their request; but sent leanness into their soul."*

David's desire to have his own way led to consequences in his life. Sometimes we "choose" the desert because we think it is an "OASIS" — like Mark in the story above. In reality, it is a MIRAGE. It is a delusion of our own making. What "appears" to be the Colorado River is a figment of our imagination. However, at other times we may know that the Lord has spoken and clearly directed our path, and yet we do not heed His direction. The end result or destination of our sinful stubbornness is the desert.

As I look at the ups and downs of my own life story and retrace the steps I have taken in my journey with Christ, I can identify many desert times or experiences. Perhaps, my primary "back side of the desert" experience took place over an 11-year period during my second pastorate in Oklahoma City, Oklahoma. Prior to moving to Oklahoma, I was a young adult ready for the second stop in my career as a pastor (so I thought!).

We had been in Kansas City for five years, and I thought it was a strategic time to move. I had been in contact with another church in Oklahoma City, and we were given an invitation to make the move and serve a new congregation. I remember attending a pastor's conference in Chicago and during my time away I began to question whether or not we should make the transition to a new setting. I thought that perhaps the Lord was stirring in my heart and wanted me to stay in our current ministry for several reasons.

I came home unconvinced and uncertain about our imminent move south. I verbalized my misgivings to my wife, and we prayed about the situation. However, in the proceeding days I made the decision to move anyway.

After we made the move, we began to encounter and experience tremendous conflict and resistance in various forms. What "appeared" to be the Colorado River was actually a "mirage" of my own making! I felt like I was in the midst of a cyclone of spiritual warfare at a level that I had never previously experienced.

In retrospect, the situation was not a "fit" for us or the new church family. The spiritual gifts, abilities and experience God had given and developed in me were not really what the church needed during that season in their life after having lost their founding pastor. My leadership style and philosophy of ministry was not congruent in many ways with the mainstream of the church leadership. Oklahoma City was a wonderful experience for my wife and children; however, it was a painful desert experience for me. God graciously gave us and the church good "seasons" within the "Season" of those eleven years. He accomplished good things.

God used the experience as a "teaching tool" in my life. He is able to work all things together for good (Romans 8:28). However, I still wonder to this day if the move at that time in our lives was God's "Plan A" for our family or simply a door that He "allowed" us to walk through in His all-knowing sovereignty. Proverbs 3:5-6 says, *"Trust in the Lord will all your heart, and do not lean on your own understanding. In all your ways acknowledge Him, and He will make straight your paths."*

The move south as a young pastor made perfect sense when analyzed. In my prideful heart, I thought I deserved what "appeared" to be a better opportunity to use "my" abilities and become better known. My "head" said yes as we prepared to move; however, my "heart" told me something else. What my heart was trying to tell me didn't make sense. Was God speaking to my heart? Likely so.

Scripture tells us to trust the Lord with all our heart and not to lean on our own common sense. It does not mean we should not use it. However, we are not to overuse it. Years later, we had another opportunity to make a move. At that time, my heart said "yes," but my head said "no." We made the move. We trusted in the Lord with all our hearts, even though we could not make sense of our circumstances intellectually.

The move we made was like God parting the waters of the Red Sea for the nation of Israel when He led them out of Egypt. By faith, we stepped into a situation where God was working. Led by His Spirit, we "fit" like a hand in a glove or piece of the puzzle into the perfect spot in His evident plan.

Supreme Sovereignty

I do not understand this fully, but I believe there are times when God in His all-knowing, supreme sovereignty will actually lead us into a desert experience. We have examples of this in both the Old and New Testaments. Think of the nation of Israel and their experience. In Exodus 13:17-18, it is clearly stated that God, in His sovereign goodness, led them into and through the desert in their journey to the land of the Canaanites, *"a land flowing with milk and honey."*

He used the desert experience to test them and to teach them, according to Deuteronomy 8:2-3. He did this knowing all the time that they would rebel in their relationship with Him once they experienced the desert! In the New Testament, we have the testimony of Jesus' life. In Matthew 4:1, we read, *"Then Jesus was led up by the Spirit into the wilderness to be tempted by the devil."* In Luke 4:1-2 we have a similar description, *"And Jesus, full of the Holy Spirit, returned from the Jordan and was led by the Spirit into the wilderness for forty days, being tempted by the devil."*

At other times, God will allow us to go through a desert time in our lives. We see numerous examples of this throughout the Bible. Job (Job 1, 20; young Daniel (Daniel 1, 3); David, a man after God's own heart (1 Samuel 19-31); and the apostle Paul (2 Corinthians 4:7-12) each had their "divinely ordained" desert times. If you study the psalms carefully, it seems that there were many times in the experience of David that God allowed him to go through a desert or dry time spiritually so that He would seek Him more fervently (Psalm 77:1-9).

I recently received the following letter from a former elder in our church. He and his wife made a move to another city after much heartfelt prayer and seeking of God before he took a new position with another company. He described his experience in painful detail.

It has been quite a year since we moved here. Actually, it's been the most difficult year I've ever experienced. The job I moved into proved extremely stressful ... taking up to 65-70 hours a week ... many times working seven days. It was overwhelming and totally consumed me. I felt like what the children of Israel must have felt with the Red Sea in front of them and the Egyptian army behind the ... an impossible situation. God gave strength, but it sure stretched us ... at times I wonder if we had made the right move. I was encouraged with the book, *God Always Makes a Way* by Robert J. Morgan. I leaned on the fact that God meant for me to be where I was ... He allows our faith to be tried, permitting trials-pressures-stress-troubles, seemingly more than we can bear ... either putting us in a difficult place or allowing us to be there for His reasons ... kind of like a refiners fire. The heat was turned up!

As things developed, I eventually resigned. We were comforted with the truth that God directs our steps and sometimes each step happens just to lead us to the next step. Once I resigned, I began looking for another job. God provided another facility within driving distance from home. I was able to move from one job to the other without a break in employment. What a blessing ... especially in this economy!

The example of this godly, well-meaning, sincere hearted couple can be multiplied endless times by each person reading this story. There are times when our sovereign God either leads us into or allows us to go through desert times. We may never fully understand all the reasons why the Lord works in His mysterious ways, but one of the results is often a deeper intimacy with the One we were created for communion with!

#3 — What Are the Effects of the Desert?

Read Psalm 63 again. Notice that there are three primary potential effects on our soul when we go through the SAHARA (desert) in our lives. We observe each of them in the three stanzas of this psalm: 1) a deeper desire for God (vv. 1-4) 2) a deeper delight in God (vv. 5-7) 3) a deeper dependence on God (vv. 8-11).

A Deeper Desire for God

(vv. 1-4)

There are three stanzas in this psalm, and in each stanza, the word "soul" is repeated to introduce a new section of the psalm (vv. 1, 5, 8). Notice the first effect this "desert experience" had on David in verses 1 to 4.

O God, you are my God; earnestly I seek you; my soul thirsts for you; my flesh faints for you, as in a dry and weary land where there is no water. So I have looked upon you in the sanctuary, beholding your power and glory. Because your steadfast love is better than life, my lips will praise you. So I will bless you as long as I live; in your name I will lift up my hands.

As David goes through this desert experience, he has a renewed desire; a deeper desire to seek after God! The dry desert experience he endures creates within his soul a desire for connection with God. David, in his inner being, has a deep thirst and hunger for communion with God. The language in this first stanza describes a person who yearns and longs for a personal, intimate, vital relationship with God. He says, *"You are my God"; "earnestly"* (early; at dawn; intensely; diligently) I seek you. This word is used many times throughout the Old Testament (Psalm 78:34; Proverbs 8:17; Isaiah 26:8, 9; Hosea 5:15).

David declares, *"my soul thirsts for you!"* This is the same metaphor used in Psalm 42:2. How often in life we look to other things and for other activities, relationships or possessions to satisfy our thirst, when only the Lord can satisfy the longings of our soul. Jesus said to the Samaritan woman at the well in Sychar, *"Everyone who drinks of this water will be thirsty again, but whoever drinks of the water that I will give him will never be thirsty again. The water that I will give him will become in him a spring of water welling up to eternal life"* (John 4:13-14).

David, in his renewed desire for communion with God, *his* God, has a renewed view of who God is! He sees God in a new way and as he saw him back in Jerusalem in the sanctuary. He sees His POWER, His GLORY and His STEADFAST LOVE (v. 2-3). The result of this deeper desire for God is praise and prayer! The Hebrew word for praise in this verse connotes addressing God in a loud tone. His *"steadfast love"* is better than earthly life (Philippians 1:21, 23)! So he breaks into praise and lifts his hands to the Lord, which was the typical Jewish posture for prayer. He "blesses" God, an act of kneeling adoration.

During my "desert experience" described earlier, I was often drawn to the Lord in prayer and praise as He began to teach me that He was the One I was to seek rather than the achievements of a career or the accomplishments of the vocational ministry. I still remember entering our sanctuary and singing hymns of worship in intimate communion with my Lord. I vividly remember one humid, sweltering summer day when I walked into the church sanctuary. From the dry thirst of my soul I began to pray and sing. The words of one of Bernard Clairvaux's beloved hymns leapt from the page of the hymnal, lit a fire of passion in my heart and brought tears of gratitude to my soul as I wept the words of, "O Sacred Head Now Wounded."

O SACRED HEAD NOW WOUNDED

O sacred Head, now wounded,
With grief and shame weighed down,
Now scornfully surrounded
With thorns, thine only crown:

How art thou pale with anguish,
With sore abuse and scorn!
How does that visage languish
Which once was bright as morn!

What thou, my Lord, has suffered
Was all for sinners' gain;
Mine was the transgression,
But thine the deadly pain.

Lo, here I fall, my Savior!
'Tis I deserve the place;
Look on me with thy favor,
Vouchsafe to me thy grace.

What language shall I borrow
To thank thee, dearest friend,
For this thy dying sorrow,
Thy pity without end?

O make me thine forever;
And should I fainting be,
Lord, let me never, never
Outlive my love to thee.

I will always remember the words H. D. McCarty insightfully wrote, "Life is the process of losing one thing after another. Victory is replacing what is lost with more of Christ."[2] Fire and heat are great purifiers of the soul. As we encounter dry times and endure seasons of drought, they become a tool God can use to empty our hearts of the clutter of life that crowds out Christ. Desert times, if not resisted, draw us into God's presence. They are an opportunity to replace what we lose with more of Christ.

A Deeper Delight in God

(vv. 5-7)

"My soul will be satisfied as with fat and rich food, and my mouth will praise you with joyful lips, when I remember you upon my bed, and meditate on you in the watches of the night; for you have been my help, and in the shadow of your wings I will sing for joy."

As David continues to open his soul in the second stanza, he says in verse 5, *"My soul will be satisfied."* This Hebrew word means "to fill to satisfaction." It is a word that is used 23 times in the psalms (Psalm 17:15; 36:7-8; 107:9).

Have you ever been desperately hungry and eaten a delicious meal of your favorite food so that you were filled to satisfaction? As you walked away from the table or restaurant and someone asked you how you felt, you probably said, "I am satisfied."

My wife Elizabeth loves good Mexican food (we both do). We had the opportunity to spend one fall in Waco, Texas, as I worked on my doctorate. One of the highlights of our time in Waco was eating frequently at Ninfa's Mexican Food Restaurant. Often, we would not eat much during the day so that we were ready for some good Mexican food later that evening. If you are ever in Waco, Texas, and enjoy Mexican food, make sure you make the scene at Ninfa's. It was a great eating-out experience. They pile on the food and bring you great chips, sauce, guacamole, fajitas, tacos, tamales, enchiladas, rice and beans and whatever else you like in Mexican food. When we finished and pushed back from the table, we were well satisfied!

David is consumed with God like we are when we are hungry and preoccupied with being filled with physical food! He *remembers* God and *meditates* on Him during the watches of the night. What do you remember when you wake up during the night? What do you think about? What are you mindful of? What do you mull over "mutter about" and meditate on when you wake up? This word for meditation that David chooses to describe the state of his soul in these verses is used often in other places in the psalms and Old Testament (Psalm 1:2; 35:28; 77:12; Joshua 1:8).

Look at the final verse, verse 7, in this stanza of the psalm. Notice the intimate relationship that David had with God as he describes the SATISFACTION of his SOUL in God! He is like a young child with his mother or a baby bird tucked under the wing of the mother bird. He says, *"YOU (God) have been my help. You have come to my aid"* (Psalm 108:12), and *"in the shadow of your wings I sing for joy."* The Hebrew word means "to creak" or shout for joy! This is one of David's favorite images of God's protection and care in the psalms (Psalm 17:8; 36:7; 57:1; 61:3, 4; 91:1; 121:5).

When I read these words, I'm reminded of our granddaughter, Megan. At the ripe old age of six months, she was so precious and huggable. Unfortunately, she didn't want her grandfather to be one of those hugging and holding her! Whenever I made the attempt, she would shriek and cry like I was some kind of monster. Don't you feel sorry for me?

My daughter, Heidi, comforted me with the reality that Megan related to all men in this way at this stage in her life. Megan much preferred to be around women, especially her mother. Despite being upset in the presence of a stranger that threatened her very existence, everything was made right as soon as "Mom" appeared. When she was safely in her mom's arms, she would coo like a young bird under the safety and shadow of its mother's wings. Scripture is rich and relevant in the images and metaphors it uses to communicate God's golden truth.

A Deeper Dependence on God

(vv. 8-9)

Technically, the last stanza of this beautiful song (poem) begins in verse 9. However, David introduces the last stanza in the last verse of the second stanza, verse 8!

> *My soul clings to you; your right hand upholds me. But those who seek to destroy my life shall go down into the depths of the earth; they shall be given over to the power of the sword; they shall be a portion for jackals. But the king shall rejoice in God; all who swear by him shall exult, for the mouths of liars will be stopped.*

The word used to describe "soul cling" in verse 8 means "to follow close or hard after; to catch by pursuit; to adhere to; to cleave to; to be joined together." It is the same word that describes God's prescription for the husband as he pursues intimacy with his wife in Genesis 2:24, *"Therefore a man shall leave his father and mother and hold fast to his wife, and they shall become one flesh."* This same word is used in Deuteronomy 10:20, *"You shall fear the LORD your God. You shall serve Him and hold fast to Him."*

The word is also used to describe Ruth's refusal to leave Naomi and return to her home in Moab despite Naomi's insistence that she do so. The Bible describes the tearful scene in Ruth 1:14, *"Then they lifted up their voices and wept again. And Orpah kissed her mother-in-law, but Ruth clung to her."* In 2 Kings 18:6, we have a similar description of good king Hezekiah who "held fast" to the Lord. This word describes the intimacy and love of a husband and a wife; a daughter and a mother; and a follower of Christ and his or her Lord!

In the final three verses of Psalm 63 David expresses his DEPENDENCE on the LORD and his confidence in God's DELIVERANCE from the DESERT. Part of the desert experience for David was his enemies who have sent him into exile in the wilderness of Judah. He talks about those enemies who sought to destroy his life in verses 9-11. Enemies who wish us "ill" instead of "well" are like prickly cactuses or poisonous snakes that make our stay in the desert miserable.

We have all encountered people like this during our stay in the wilderness. David says that it is the Lord's right hand that upholds him in verse 8. The imagery of God upholding us with His right hand of power is used in Isaiah 41:10, "Fear not, for I am with you; be not dismayed, for I am your God; I will strengthen you, I will help you, I will uphold you with my righteous right hand."

Closing Challenge

Michael Yaconelli, in *Messy Spirituality*, makes these observations about the Christian life and our relationship with God.

Spirituality is not a formula; it is not a test. It is a relationship. Spirituality is not about competency; it is about intimacy. Spirituality is not about perfection; it is about connection. The way of the spiritual life begins where we are now in the mess of our lives. Accepting the reality of our broken, flawed lives is the beginning of spirituality, not because the spiritual life will remove flaws, but because we let go of seeking perfection and instead seek God, the One who is present in the tangledness of our lives. Spirituality is not about being fixed; it is about God's being present in the mess of our unfixedness."[3]

What do you think God is trying to teach you about Himself at the present time? Take some time *now* to evaluate your own life. Make a list of some of the desert experiences you have endured. Perhaps you are presently experiencing the heat of the desert. How did you get there? Why do you think God allowed this "wilderness way" to be a part of your spiritual journey? How do you think God wants to use these experiences "in the mess of your unfixedness"?

My father and father-in-law are both traveling through the lonely desert of losing their brides, the love of their lives. They both enjoyed joyful healthy loving relationships with their dear wives for about sixty years. Sometimes we never fully understand why the Lord allows certain deserts to come our way this side of heaven. All we can do is surrender and draw closer to Him, the One who loves us and desires a closer relationship with us.

The following poem was part of my father-in-law's journey during his service to our country in Burma during World War II. It is still a description of his journey as he grows deeper in his relationship with God today.

"THIS PATH"

He chose this path for thee,
Though well He knew sharp thorns would tear thy feet,
Knew well how the brambles would obstruct the way,

Knew all the hidden dangers thou wouldst meet,
Knew how thy faith would falter day by day,
And still the whisper echoes, "Yes, this path is best for thee."[4]

Chapter 7

THE DOORWAY TO INTIMACY

THE ROLE OF
THE SAVIOR (REVELATION 2:1-7)

S everal years ago I read a story that described the singular love of King Louis IX of France for his wife Margaret. As a young man, he married princess Margaret of Province. On his wedding ring he had the following words engraved: *"God, France, Margaret."* He would often say, "I have no love outside this ring." Some believe that this was the secret of his being known in history as Saint Louis.[1]

This story reminds me of our annual observance of Valentine's Day — the day for communicating and renewing our love for the one we are devoted to. In 2010, Valentine's Day fell on Sunday for the first time in eleven years. As a pastor, I obviously track things by Sundays! The last time this special day occurred on a Sunday, which it rarely does, was 1999. Valentine's Day is all about pursuing intimacy with your spouse. It is about telling that special person you love that they are the priority of your life. It is a day to communicate again what you feel about that person. It is a time to recommit to what you committed to when you married that guy or gal who captured your heart. It is an opportunity for tilling the tender soil of your heart and cultivating a vital, personal relationship with that person.

The images of King Louis IX and Valentine's Day can also be symbols of our relationship with the SAVIOR. God sent the human race the very first Valentine's Day card when He sent us His Son, our Savior. The apostle John describes God's Valentine's-like love for us in John 3:16, with the words that so many of us have etched on the table of our hearts, *"For God so loved the world, that he gave His only Son, that whoever believes in Him should not perish but have eternal life."*

It is in the Son we have life and through Him that we find a relationship with God the Father. If the first priority in life is cultivating this intimate relationship, then it is essential to talk about the One who opens the door for the pursuit of that relationship.

To this point, we have been examining different means God uses to enable us to experience intimacy in our relationship with Him. We have been exploring some of the "tools" the Father uses to deepen that relationship. In Chapter 2, we discovered the tool of *solemnity* (getting serious!) as we looked at God's message through the prophet Joel and his call to hold a sacred assembly. In Chapter 3, we talked about the topic of *sin*, the primary obstacle to intimacy. In Chapter 4, we immersed ourselves in the experience of *suffering*, the shared struggle of every human person. In Chapter 5, the theme was *sadness*. God can use times of darkness and depression to draw us deeper in our relationship with Christ. Chapter 6 centered on the image of *Sahara* as a metaphor for dry times or desert experiences, which can create an inner thirst for God. In the next chapter, we will examine the reality of *setbacks* (failure and disappointment), another one of those unwanted experiences common to all of us. However, before we go any further it is important to pause, catch our breath and look at Christ.

It would be unforgivable in our quest for intimacy with God if we did not center this journey in the Savior. After all, He is the "Center" of the journey. He is the "author and finisher" of our faith. He is the One who makes the expedition possible. In fact, the only way we can have intimacy with God is by pursuing intimacy with THE SAVIOR, our Lord Jesus Christ. Pursuing intimacy with God is all about pursuing intimacy with CHRIST.

Jesus referred to this relationship in John 14:6, *"I am the way, and the truth and the life. No one comes to the Father except through me."* He described it again, in John 17:3, *"And this eternal life, that you know the only true God, and Jesus Christ whom you have sent."* The apostle Paul described his quest for this relationship when he said, *"Indeed, I count everything as loss because of the surpassing worth of knowing Christ Jesus my Lord"* (Philippians 3:8).

There can be no intimacy with God without a personal, intimate, vital relationship with Jesus Christ.

Falling In and Out of Love

Is your spiritual journey with Jesus anything like mine? Are there times in this trip toward intimacy that you have fallen out of love with Christ? Have there been other seasons when your love for the Savior has burned brightly as you grew in your knowledge of Him and your passion to obey Him?

I can remember times when my knowing of Christ deepened dramatically and other seasons when the flame of love and desire for a growing relationship with Him began to flicker and grow faint. The journey toward intimacy with God and Christ is a lot like a road trip that takes us around unexpected curves, uphill climbs and sharp descents into unwanted valleys.

When we find the flame flickering and the valley looming how do we renew our love relationship with Christ? I think that Revelation 2:1-7 give us some answers to this question we all struggle with at times.

How Do We Renew Our Love Relationship With Jesus Christ?

So how do we keep it fresh? How do we make sure that we are pursuing life's first priority of cultivating a personal, intimate, vital relationship with Christ? If you study this passage carefully, then it is clear that the believers in the church at Ephesus were in danger of losing that love relationship. The Lord recounts their virtues and attributes in verse 2. Then He goes on to say, *"But I have this against you, that you have abandoned the love you had at first."* The Greek word "to abandon" in Revelation 2:4 means "to let go; to give up; to forsake or to lay aside."

For whatever the reason, their love relationship (intimacy with Christ) was slipping away. In an effort to help them re-kindle that love, the Lord Jesus Christ (referred to 1:12-20) does four things. First, He COMMENDS them (vv. 2-3, 6); then He CORRECTS them (v. 4); He COUNSELS them as He gives them a RECIPE for RENEWAL (v. 5a); and finally, He CAUTIONS them (v. 5b). He gives them the consequences of their actions if they choose to stay on the same course — traveling in the same direction and doing the same things.

Notice the first thing our Lord does in this love letter that He sends to the church at Ephesus. He COMMENDS them; He does not CONDEMN them! Wow!! Our **Omnipotent** (all-powerful; He holds the angels *"in His right hand!"* 1:16, 20; 2:1); **Omnipresent** (ever-present; *"He is 'among' the seven golden lampstands!"* 1:13, 2:1); **Omniscient** (all-knowing; *"I know your works!"* 2:1) Lord knows everything about us — good and bad! He knows our beauty marks and blemishes (just as He did the Church at Ephesus). He knows our strengths and our weaknesses; and yet, the first thing He does is commend us! The all powerful, present-everywhere, all-knowing God who knows our deeds begins by commending us instead of condemning us!

I am reminded of Jesus words in John 3:17, immediately after God's Valentine message, *"For God did not send His Son into the world to condemn the world, but in order that the world might be saved through Him."*

His Commendation

Revelation 2:2-3, 6

Notice what He commends in the church at Ephesus. He commends their faithfulness to the TASK (vv. 2a, 3) and the TRUTH (vv. 2b, 6). The Apostle John wrote Revelation from the Isle of Patmos off the coast of Asia Minor around 95 A.D. The Revelation was written approximately sixty-five years after Christ's crucifixion and more than thirty years after Paul's ministry in Ephesus. These Christians had been faithful to the task of proclaiming the good news about Christ and serving Him all of those years. They had zealously guarded and protected the truth of the faith against those who wanted to twist it, pervert it and undermine it.

The Lord says in Revelation 2:2-3, *"'I know your works, your toil and your patient endurance, and how you cannot bear with those who are evil, but have tested those who call themselves apostles and are not, and found them to be false. I know you are enduring patiently and bearing up for my name's sake, and you have not grown weary.'"*

He commends them again in verse 6, *"You hate the work of the Nicolaitans, which I also hate."* The Nicolaitans were a heretical Christian sect that perverted the doctrine of grace and turned it into license to do whatever you want (Revelation 2:14-15; Romans 6:1-4, 12-14, 15).

The Church at Ephesus reminds me of the life of "George Bailey" in the movie classic, *It's a Wonderful Life*. Is your family like ours? Almost every Christmas, when the kids were growing up, we would watch this all-time favorite with Jimmie Stewart and Donna

Reed. Despite watching it numerous times, I would find tears welling up in my eyes at the end of the movie when George was recognized for his good deeds, and Harold, the angel, finally got his wings.

George Bailey was the guy we all hope that we can be or become during our lifetime. He faithfully, tirelessly, and selflessly served others in his family and community, all the while, consistently denying himself of dreams and desires he wanted to pursue.

If you have your Bible open, notice the description of these early believers. The Church at Ephesus was the "George Bailey" of the ancient world. They were an example to the other churches in Asia Minor of hard working, loyal endurance in serving Christ and courageous perseverance in standing for the truth against those who would twist it. The "descriptions" in these verses remind me of the church I am currently serving and the many leaders who have faithfully served Christ over the past 38 years since the inception of the church.

His Correction

Revelation 2:4

As your read this you may be feeling pretty good about yourself! Who doesn't want to be like George Bailey? I have always admired him. We all cheer for him and cry for him when we watch the movie. What woman would not like to be Donna Reed and be married to a guy like Jimmie Stewart on Valentine's Day.

However, notice that the Lord has something against the Church at Ephesus. He goes on to challenge and correct them! They were orthodox but they were not on fire in their intimate love relationship with the Lord. The flame of their first love was not burning, *"But I have this against you, that you have abandoned the love you had at first."* Most English translations render this last phrase in

Revelation 2:4, *"Your first (chief, foremost in order of importance, priority) love."* Despite all of their commendable qualities, the one thing that the Lord critiques is the condition of their heart!

Somewhere in the midst of all their faithful service and tireless work, things had become routine, rote, and mundane. The lives of these followers of Christ had taken on the flair of George Bailey's life — faithful but mundane. The excitement and love they had when they first gave their lives to Christ was no longer there. God desires orthodoxy but He delights in "orthopraxy"! Somehow in their pursuit of all these other good attributes (vv. 2-3) they had "laid aside" or "let go of" what should have been their first priority!

Many couples experience this kind of thing in their marriages, don't they? (Scripture uses the analogy of marriage as a description of our relationship with Christ in Ephesians 5:21-33.)

We have all been to weddings and emotionally participated in that special moment when the unity candle is lit by the adoring couple following the exchange of their vows and rings. Do you know of any couples who step to the altar on their wedding day, light the unity candle as a symbol of their covenant, while simultaneously planning to fall out of love? Obviously, the thought of lighting the unity candle and planning to abandon one's vows is absurd.

However, somehow and somewhere along the way the flame begins to flicker and the fire goes out in the marriage relationship of many couples. Between the altar and the door of the church, on the marriage journey of buying a home, having children and getting established in a career, the pursuit of intimacy with our spouse often wanes.

How or Why?

If we use the metaphor of marriage as a picture or our relationship with Christ, then the immediate question I have is *why*? Why do we lose the love we had when we first came to Christ? How does it happen?

There are many reasons, perhaps too many to discuss in one brief chapter. However, here are a few of the more obvious reasons common to all of us that come to my mind.

Duty

I think sometimes we lose our love for the Lord when doing our "duty" for Christ takes the place of knowing Christ and being with Christ! As one man has said so well, "Loving devotion for Christ can be lost in the midst of active service to Christ."[2] This is the insidious disease of vocational ministry and Christian leadership. It is also the subtle deception that invades the heart of many long-time followers of Christ.

Remember the story of Martha and Mary in Luke 10:38-42? Martha was consumed with her duty to serve the Lord, which became a barrier to enjoying her relationship with the Lord. Jesus answer to her preoccupation with service sticks like a sharp arrow in her soul, *"Martha, Martha, you are anxious and troubled about many things, but one thing is necessary. Mary has chosen the good portion, which will not be taken away from her"* (Luke 10:41-42).

At the end of the day and at the beginning of eternity, *"sitting at the Lord's feet to listen"* is far more important than duty-bound service for Christ.

One of my greatest struggles in vocational ministry is the constant pressure of putting duty to ministry *for* Christ before my relationship *with* Christ. Can you identify? When we make the "Martha Mistake" and fall into the frantic "service syndrome," then what began out of loving devotion becomes an insidious idolatry of our duty. The "Martha Mistake" empties our soul of joy and energy.

Why do we seem to constantly gravitate back to being a Martha instead of a Mary and repeat the same mistake? Why do you think we do this?

Busy

There are also those times when we can lose our love for the Lord because we are too busy pursuing other pursuits and shallow priorities. This is the subtle deception of the age we are living in. In our affluent, leisure-oriented, "you deserve a break today," high-tech, "more is better," "faster is best" age, it is easy to crowd Christ out of our lives!

This may have been the main problem with the believers in Ephesus. They were constantly bombarded with all the choices offered them living in the in the strategic metropolis ("Vanity Fair") of Ephesus, with the Temple of Artemis, one of the seven wonders of the ancient world. Gordon MacDonald alluded to this problem years ago in *Ordering Your Private World*. He described leisure as "cotton candy for the soul."[3]

In America (and many other Western countries), we live in a society where the leisure and technology industries have created what I call "pseudo-rest." We exhaust ourselves physically and emotionally, as well as empty ourselves spiritually, in our endless, busy pursuit of all the choices that our leisure and technology offer us.

Are you like me and my family? Do you find yourself bombarded by choices that pull you away from pursuing intimacy with God (the One who satisfies our soul) toward the "deception" that the other "busy pursuits" of life will bring you the satisfaction you yearn for?

Complacency

Sometimes we can lose our love for Christ because we have had it too good for too long. Affluence, leisure and "technology overload"[4] can lead to complacency. The believers John was writing to were the second generation of believers in Ephesus (A.D. 95). The first generation of pioneers that met with Paul for three years was gone (Acts 19-20). The torch had been passed, and the fire was going out! It is easy for that to happen, is it not? In the midst of our comfort, we become complacent and lose sight of Christ!

Complacency can be a form of laziness. When I become complacent in my life, I begin to coast in the regular exercise of some of the basic spiritual disciplines that are "means of grace" for my soul, as Dallas Willard or Donald Whitney would describe them.[5] God doesn't want us to pursue spiritual disciplines like prayer, reading and meditating on Scripture, or the practice of solitude as a means to an end in a legalistic manner.

However, if pursued in the right spirit and with the goal of connecting and communicating with God because I need Him to survive and thrive, then they are vital to our spiritual well-being. Complacency that leads to lethargy can kill my quest for a deeper relationship with the Lord who loves me and yearns to have a relationship with me.

One of the stories that I read early in my Christian journey was the story entitled *My Heart — Christ's Home*. Have you read the story? I can still picture in my mind's eye the main character in Robert Boyd Munger's classic booklet as he rushes out the door one morning with the Lord sitting in the den by the fireplace waiting to commune and communicate with him. The duties and busyness of his life had led to the flickering and waning of his loving devotion to Christ. Spiritual complacency led to a lethargy that led to little pursuit of intimacy with his Lord.

In the story, the man glances over his shoulder in his stressful rush out the door. As he glances he sees the Lord sitting there. He pauses to ask Jesus a question and discovers that He has been there every morning waiting for renewed communication and connection with His child. The conversation leads to the man stopping that day and sitting down to converse with his Lord.

That brief glance and the conversation that followed changed his routine and his life. The days ahead were different as he renewed his first love and began to pursue an intimate, personal, vital relationship with the Savior who alone can satisfy our soul. Notice Christ's counsel to us. He gives us a recipe for renewal in our relationship with Christ.

His Counsel

Revelation 2:5

Notice that the Lord is not out to condemn us. He is out to help us! He gives us some wise counsel in verse 5. The Lord gives us His recipe for renewal of our love relationship with the Lord who loves us and longs to commune with us when He says, "Remember, therefore, from where you have fallen; repent, and do the works you did at first." Let's look carefully at this recipe for renewal.

Remember!

The word "remember" means to "exercise your memory" which is the opposite of complacency. In order to "remember," you have to sweep the attic of your mind and dust off the mental cobwebs. The Greek word can mean to rehearse or be mindful, which is hard work. It is a command, not an option. It is in the present tense. We are to remember and keep on remembering. Remembering is a discipline. We are to practice looking back and remembering!

Remember what it was like when you first began your relationship with the Lord! Do you remember your excitement about the Lord? Do you remember your hunger for His Word? Do you remember the desire for fellowship with His people? Do you remember your passion for worship?

Write down your reflections! Establish a baseline of how it was and what it was like! The baseline becomes a goal. The way it was is the way it should be — only deeper and better! Sometimes spiritual decline, like marital decline, is very subtle, and we don't even know it is happening! The "flame" of loving intimacy becomes a flicker and the fire goes out — unless we practice remembering!

My wonderful wife, who has a mind for detail and a much better memory than I do, often asks me, *"Do you remember?"* When she asks me that question, I often get irritated and impatient because the question always challenges me to think back and reflect on events or conversations long-since forgotten.

However, after my initial irritation when she reminds me of what she is talking about, I am almost always glad she did. There is a reason she asks me to remember. It is usually for my good, the family's well-being or the growth of our marriage. It is helpful to "call to mind" important events or past lessons I thought I learned but then realize I have forgotten. Thank God for my wife who challenges me to remember the things that I need to remember. I am a better person and our relationship is deeper and more vital because of it.

Repent!

The next thing Jesus does is to call us to repent! The Greek word for repentance means "to reconsider or to think differently." When you repent you "change your mind" about the way you think about life or your priorities. The command here is in the aorist tense. Repentance is a decision. It is an act of the will that results in a change of heart and life (practice).

We do not necessarily have to be living in sin or even pursuing sin before we repent. When we repent, we have a change in our understanding. We change the way we are looking at things, the value we are placing on things, and the direction we are heading in life. When we repent, we turn around and start going back to where we began. We start putting first things first! The most important things become the most important things. Sometimes it takes a "crisis" to bring us to the point where we are willing to have a change of mind and heart. It takes things like suffering, sadness, Sahara, and *setbacks* (which we will talk about in the next chapter). However, it is the Spirit of God that enables us to make this change.

My second daughter, Jennifer, and her husband Matt were married on the fourth of July seven years ago. They had one of those "fairy tale" kinds of weddings. They were married outdoors at Glen Eyrie, the headquarters of the Navigators in Colorado Springs, Colorado. They rode in a carriage around the grounds of the idyllic castle estate following the ceremony. They assumed that their fairytale wedding would lead to a fairytale life!

When they were married, they exchanged wedding bands as most couples do. On the inside of their wedding bands, they had the following words engraved, *"To God be the Glory"* in Swahili, the native tongue of Tanzania, Africa. They had talked for hours about the possibility of someday serving the Lord in Tanzania. The possibility of serving the Lord in Africa has been a long-time dream of Matt's, and it was embraced by my adventuresome daughter. Last year, they made a fact-finding trip to Tanzania after months of planning and anticipation. Inexplicably (at the time) and surprisingly, Jennifer became violently sick and subsequently experienced severe anxiety. The circumstance led to great stress and hours of counseling. Without relating all the details, this led to a halt in their plans, a shortened trip, a visit to the doctor and a long journey of recovery for my daughter. Obviously, the circumstance affected Matt, their marriage and the entire family, including their children.

It has been a long time since this unwanted, unanticipated "visitor" of anxiety knocked on the door of my daughter's heart and mind. However, today they would both tell you that they would not trade the days of darkness and weeks of pain for anything. They have learned truths about themselves, their marriage, their family and life, which they would not have learned apart from this "crisis." Through their suffering, sadness, and Sahara experience, they are learning that it is not God and Africa (something else) but that God ALONE is their "FULL PORTION." Matt will often make this statement. He is learning that the Lord is to be his full portion. They are discovering their full satisfaction in their relationship with Him and their surrender to His agenda for their lives. It is all about Him and His Glory!

Sometimes a change of mind and heart is painful. Often, God allows us to go through painful experiences to soften our hearts, cause us to remember and bring us to the point of wanting or being willing to change. This has certainly been the case in my own stubborn, willful, driven and duty-bound relationship with Christ. Sadly, I could fill the pages of this book and many more with my own stories of how the Lord, in His loving, relentless pursuit of a relationship with me, allowed similar "crises" in my life to bring me to the bittersweet place of thinking and living differently.

Repeat!

The third and final step in the Lord's recipe for renewal for us is to return. When we return we "go back" to those things that we were doing at first (when we first fell in love with the Lord) and repeat them! The Lord says in verse 5, *"Do the things you did at first!"* Literally we are to "do the first works." Doing or repeating what we used to do is devotion. In the Christian life, we never graduate from first grade! No matter how mature we may be (or think we may be), we need to always revisit, repeat and keep repeating the foundational disciplines of the Christian faith which I mentioned earlier.

When was the last time you picked up an older book like Dallas Willard's *The Spirit of the Disciplines*, Daniel Whitney's *Spiritual Disciplines for the Christian Life*, Richard Foster's *Celebration of Discipline* or William Law's *A Serious Call to a Devout and Holy Life* (a bit legalistic in my opinion)? Books like these can often be a tool (if you enjoy reading) which God can use to encourage us in the practice of repeating the things that we did at first in our relationship with Christ.

This side of heaven, we never grow beyond our need of repetition. Living the Christian life means enrollment in the lifelong school of Christ. Being a fully devoted follower of Christ means being devoted to the goal of being a lifelong learner. Being a lifelong learner or lover of Christ means repetition until our graduation day into His presence when we will finally see Him as He is — face to face — with full and complete intimacy and joy!

Think about marriage again for a moment. Often in marriage, we stop practicing the very things that led us to fall in love when we were dating. Typically, after we have been married for a while, the practices that enabled us to grow closer together are neglected and taken for granted as we coast or drift into complacency and away from intimacy. In our busyness, we unintentionally neglect life's most important earthly relationship. Out of duty to other things, we stop doing the things we should be doing if our marriage is a priority.

However, in a healthy personal, intimate, vital marriage relationship, you are *always* dating, *always* communicating, *always* listening, *always* confessing, forgiving and repenting! When we are practicing (doing) these "basic" disciplines it is an expression of our ongoing, intimate devotion to that person we married and "say" we love. Isn't it the same in our love relationship with the Lord?

His Caution

Revelation 2:5b

In closing, notice that the Lord warns us! He cautions us! He tells us that if we do not follow His recipe for renewal, then there will come a time when He will visit us and remove our lampstand from its place. He says, *"If not, I will come to you and remove your lampstand from its place, unless you repent"* (Revelation 2:5b).

Notice the progression or pattern in this passage. First, the flame of love began to flicker. Then the light went out, and the lampstand was removed. That is what happened in Ephesus despite all their blessings and privileges. Both the apostle Paul and John were their pastors, yet their lampstand was still removed! Today, much of this area of the world sits in the darkness of disconnection with God rather than the light of passionate love for Christ. It can happen to the best of us. What happened in Ephesus can happen to any of us if we do not heed the Lord's counsel and follow His recipe for renewal.

Closing Challenge

"Behold, I stand at the door and knock.
If anyone hears my voice and opens the door,
I will come in to him and eat with him, and he with me."

Just a few pages over in your Bible, these words stand etched in Scripture. These familiar words are Christ's invitation to another church, the church of Laodecia, in the same region as the church of Ephesus. They, too, had grown placid and complacent in their relationship with the Lord.

This invitation is forever engraved on the pages of Scripture as a reminder and an invitation to each of us. This verse is the Lord's loving invitation to open the door of our heart and step back into communion and intimacy with Him! He is there. He is always waiting, always inviting and always hoping that we will desire intimate conversation over dinner.

What steps does God want you to take as a result of reading this chapter and studying this passage? What is His word to you? Where are you in your relationship with Christ today? Are you too duty bound to sit at his feet? Perhaps you are too busy pursuing other priorities to pursue a deeper relationship with the Lord? Have you drifted into complacency in your communion with Christ? What ingredient in His recipe for renewal spoke to your heart? Does He want you to take the step of remembering? Remembering may not be your problem. Maybe the step of repenting or repeating is where you are in this season of your life.

As I close this chapter I vividly remember a moment almost forty years ago. I was in a large auditorium in Wichita, Kansas. I was going through a season of renewal in my own relationship with the Lord. The occasion was a large evangelistic event hosted by our church and led by a youth group called "All God's Children." On stage at the conclusion of the musical concert, a young girl closed with a song of invitation. I have forgotten her name.

Who knows where she is, what she is doing today or where she is in her relationship with Christ? However, on that occasion, she was chosen to close the concert. She passionately sang her song accompanied by the lone instrument she carried and played. As she fervently sang the words of Revelation 3:20, she softly strummed the strings on the guitar she gripped so tightly.

The song was a song she had personally written. To my knowledge it was never published. The song never did make it into a chorus or song book. However, the passion of her ballad penetrated the soft tissue of my spiritual heart that day. It is a song and invitation that I have carried with me and think of often when I drift in my pursuit of intimacy with Christ. I wish I could sing it for you. The words and music still echo in my memory. Do you know the words? Can you hear the music?

> *"Behold, I stand at the door and knock.*
> *If anyone hears my voice and opens the door,*
> *I will come in to him and eat with him, and he with me."*

Chapter 8

MOUNTAIN TOPS AND VALLEYS

THE TORMENT OF SETBACKS AND TRIUMPH OF SUCCESSES (PSALM 30)

P astor and author, Dr. John Piper makes this observation about life in his book *A Sweet and Bitter Providence*:

> Life is not a straight line leading from one blessing to the next then finally to heaven. Life is a winding and troubled road. Switchback after switchback. And the point of the biblical stories like Joseph and Job and Esther and Ruth is to help us feel in our bones (not just know in our heads) that God is for us in all these strange turns. God is not just showing up after trouble and cleaning it up. He is plotting the course and managing the troubles with far-reaching purposes for our good and for the glory of Jesus Christ.[1]

I lived in two different places in my early to middle school years. We lived in Colorado Springs, Colorado, as I already mentioned. I also lived in San Jose, Costa Rica after my father sold his business and moved the family to Central America. One of the things that I remember about both places was the incredible mountains that surrounded both cities. Of course, nothing can compare to the Colorado Rockies and Pikes Peak, which proudly stared at us through our breakfast window each morning while living at 2314 Lockhaven Drive in Colorado Springs. However, the lush green mountain vistas of Costa Rica, with coffee farms and colorful ox carts traveling the narrow mountain roads were a close second.

In both places, our family would often take road trips. While in Colorado, we would frequently make trips to the panhandle of west Texas to visit my grandparents or into the mountains for leisure. In Costa Rica, we made trips into the mountains to visit coffee farms and watch Irazu, an active volcano, which spewed *senesa* (gray volcanic ash) like snow over the city of San Jose almost daily.

Both in the Rockies and in the mountains of Central America, we would often make breathtaking climbs, negotiate sharp narrow curves and make rapid descents into valleys and forests. Life is like this. Life is very much like a road trip with climbs, followed by descents, accompanied by sharp unexpected bends and curves in the road. This leads me to three observations about this road trip we make between the cradle and the grave.

#1) Life Is a Journey: Webster's Dictionary defines a journey as, "Travel or passage from one place to another — a trip." Every one of us has taken a trip. We have all taken a journey, many journeys, and perhaps even too many journeys from point A to point B. We have made trips like our family did when I was a child. You have made roads trips to your house, to the home of your son, daughter, mother or father or for a vacation destination you always wanted to visit. We are all on a journey from birth to death that takes us from infancy through childhood to the teen years, adulthood and beyond.

#2) Life Is a Journey Made Up of Setbacks and Successes: Life is like a road trip filled with four-lane highways and two-lane dirt roads. It is a trip filled with good pavement and potholes. It has its peaks and valleys. It often includes long stretches of smooth, straight highway and other sections with sharp mountain curves like those in Colorado, Costa Rica or California. Our trip up the Pacific coast on old Highway 1 a few years ago, for our 30th anniversary, is a memory we will never forget. Life is like the Pacific Coast Highway. It is a journey filled with setbacks and successes. There are times when we are crashing and times when we are coasting. There is an ebb and flow to life. There are times when the tide is coming in and times when the tide is going out. Webster defines a "setback" as a "reverse, defeat, delay, a checking of progress." Setbacks are a reverse of fortune. We have all had them. One moment you think you are soaring north only to discover the next day you are sailing south. This leads me to the third observation.

#3) Life Is a Journey Made Up of Setbacks and Successes So We Learn to Find Our Satisfaction in the Savior: I truly believe that God has designed our journey through life in this way so we will learn to find our SATISFACTION in the SAVIOR. I think that was David's situation when he wrote Psalm 30, the basis of this chapter. Notice the inscription that introduces yet another psalm of David, a man after God's own heart, who often yearned for intimacy with His God during his earthly journey: A PSALM OF DAVID. A SONG AT THE DEDICATION OF THE TEMPLE.

David wrote this Psalm as a song of thanksgiving and praise at a time of deliverance and celebration in his life. He wrote this when he was succeeding. However, he wrote it after a season of setbacks and suffering. Look carefully at verses 1-3. Read the verses and let the words sink into your soul. In this psalm, David gives us a picture of the ups and downs in life's journey and his pursuit of intimacy with God in the mix. C. H. Spurgeon introduces Psalm 30 with these words.

Throughout this psalm there are indications that David had been greatly afflicted directly and indirectly, after having, in his presumption (pride) fancied himself secure. When God's children prosper one way, they are generally tried another, for few of us can bear unmingled prosperity. Even the joys of hope need to be mixed with the pains of experience, and the more surely so when comfort breeds carnal security and self-confidence.[2]

Notice the contrasting images of *"weeping and joy"* (v. 5), *"night and morning"* (v. 5), *"prosperity and dismay"* (v. 6), *"mourning and dancing"* (v. 11), *"sackcloth and gladness"* (v. 11). We do not know for sure what season of life David was in when he wrote this psalm. Spurgeon thinks that he wrote the psalm in the later days of his life — looking back (2 Chronicles 21:18-22:19). He had survived the caves in the Judean wilderness running from Saul and the setback of pridefully counting Israel by taking a census to measure the greatness of his nation, which resulted in God's discipline (1 Chronicles 21). God had mercy on David after this prideful step in the midst of his prosperity (success), and it is God's mercy and deliverance after this misstep that became the catalyst for this psalm (21:13). This psalm is like Hezekiah's song after his illness (Isaiah 38:10-20). It was used by postexilic Israel (2nd Temple) and also at the temple dedication (165 B. C.). Psalm 30 was fitting for a celebration because David was soaring north after sailing south.

As the psalm opens, we find him breaking into enthusiastic celebration over what God has done. He begins like a singer on a stage belting his solo to all who will listen. Then he invites the audience to join in the celebration and sing along with him.

David's Celebration

(vv. 1-5)

I will extol you, O Lord, for you have drawn me up and have not let my foes rejoice over me. O Lord my God, I cried to you for help, and you have healed me. O Lord, you have brought up my soul

from Sheol; you restored me to life from among those who go down to the pit.
Solo (vv. 1-3)

David opens this psalm by praising God for His deliverance from the difficulty he had experienced. He extols or exalts God. He lifts Him up for His deliverance from the setbacks he had experienced. He makes three statements in this solo of praise!

You delivered me!

David sings, *"I will exalt you, O LORD, for you have drawn me up and have not let my foes rejoice over me."* The Hebrew word he uses here means "to draw up out of deep water or to let down a bucket for drawing out water." This same term is used to describe Moses drawing up water from the well in Midian to water the flock for the seven daughters of Reuel (Exodus 2:16, 19). It is also used in Proverbs 20:5 where the writer says, *"The purpose in a man's heart is like deep water, but a man of understanding will draw it out."*

Sometimes when we are soaring along and succeeding in life and we experience a setback, it is like you end up at the bottom of a well. The only way up or out will be if someone "draws you out with a bucket." God delivered David out of his distress!

You healed me!

David then proclaims, *"O Lord my God, I cried to you for help, and you have healed me."* Notice the increase in intensity and intimacy as David sings this solo of praise and thanksgiving. When we are at the bottom of the well in the middle of some setback in our lives, it is excruciatingly painful.

Have you ever felt like David? *"I cried (shout) to you for help!"* David says that the Lord healed him. The Hebrew word means "to mend by stitching" or to make whole. Mending is a painstaking process much like quilting, knitting or crocheting. Mending is a repair job that often takes time. Often, we want a "quick fix." We want God to mend us and to do it right now! However, if we are patient, at the end of the process our LORD "mends" us if we cry to Him for help.

This imagery of mending or healing is used frequently in the psalms.[3] This is what God did for King Hezekiah when he *"wept bitterly"* before the Lord and cried out for healing when he was struck with his deathly sickness (Isaiah 38:1-5).

You restored me!

David concludes his solo, *"O Lord, you have brought up my soul from Sheol; you restored me to life from among those who go down to the pit."* The word "restore" means to revive or to bring back to life! When we are in the pit, a dungeon, a deep well or a hole of despair after a setback, sometimes we do not feel like life will ever be normal again. We have a God who revives us when we cry out to Him.

I recall a story about J. C. Penney early in his career. His experience was much like David's experience. Penney had more than his share of successes but he also went through some setbacks during his life.

In 1929, J.C. Penny's business was highly unstable. As a result, he began to worry and became sleepless. He worried to such an extreme that he contracted the shingles, the severest pain known to man. In the hospital, Penney was given medicine to tranquilize him, but it was no help. He chronically worried about his business.

One night, he felt he would die before the morning, and so he started writing farewells to his wife, son and friends. But by the next morning, as he was lying on his bed, he heard singing from the hospital chapel next door: The words of the familiar hymn, "God Will Take Care of You" came softly through the wall, "No matter what may be the test, God will take care of you … ."

Suddenly he sat up thinking: "It is real! God loves and cares for me." In an instant, he jumped out of his bed and entered the chapel. Then a miracle took place in his soul, as if he were a little bird suddenly freed to fly out of the dungeon into the sunlight, from hell to paradise.[4]

In the opening verses of Psalm 30, it is as if David jumps out of his hospital bed as he is delivered by God. He breaks out into song after God restores his life from the pit that he endured.

I think there are several life lessons about setbacks that we can glean from David's recounting of his experience in this wonderful song. Here in David's opening solo we learn our first lesson.

Lesson #1 — God Is With You in Setbacks

Sing praises to the Lord, O you his saints, and give thanks to his holy name. For his anger is but for a moment, and his favor is for a lifetime. Weeping may tarry for the night, but joy comes with the morning.
Chorus (vv. 4, 5)

After his opening solo, David invites the congregation to join in singing with him. Notice David's confidence in God in verse 5. God will bring us through valley times in His perfect time. His timeline is often not our timeline, but He will be with us and will deliver us. In Psalm 37:23-25 David reassures us from his experience, *"The steps of a man are established by the Lord, when He delights in his way; though he fall, he shall not be cast headlong, for the Lord upholds his hand. I have been young, and now am old, yet I have not seen the righteous forsaken or his children begging for bread."*

In the margin of his Bible, George Mueller, that great man of faith who established a prolific ministry to orphans in nineteenth-century England wrote next to, *"The steps of a man are established by the Lord"* the phrase, "The stops, too!"[5] God superintends our steps as we ascend and succeed in life. He also oversees the "stops" in life when we are experiencing the difficulty related to "setbacks" which He sovereignly allows.

When, not if, God brings you out of setback experiences, praise Him in the closet when you are alone. However, do not forget to share what He has done with others and invite them to sing praise with you. The Hebrew word for praise at the beginning of verse four is an orchestral instrumental word. It means "to touch the strings or parts of a musical instrument or to play or make music accompanied by the voice. The second term translated "give thanks" is used frequently in the book of Psalms and means "to hold out the hand or to worship with extended hands" to His holy name!

Sometimes in the midst of a setback, we feel like God is angry with us and our setback experience will go on forever. That is how David felt after he made the stupid, prideful mistake of taking a census of his people in order to quantify his "military might" even though Joab tried to dissuade him (1 Chronicles 21:1-5). Whether we are going through a difficulty due to God's discipline (like David — read 1 Chronicles 21) or some form of distress which God has allowed for some unknown reason, we often think that we will never get beyond it. We think what many before us have thought, "Life will be this way forever."

However, notice again what David says based on his experience. *"Weeping may tarry for the night, but joy comes with the morning."* Sadness and sorrow may come and "dwell" or make their home during the darkness (at dusk) but joy *comes* (not "might" come) at the dawn — as surely as the sun comes up! Actually, there is no verb in the Hebrew text. The thought is parallel to the thought at the beginning of the phrase. Just as weeping tarries or lodges so joy comes in the morning!

Frequently, I am encouraged and ministered to through *Our Daily Bread* devotional ministry of RBC (Radio Broadcast Company). Recently, I read a helpful analogy from the pen of the late Joanie Yoder who encouraged so many in their journey with Christ over the years.

> I'll never forget my first experience using an automatic car wash. Approaching it with the dread of going to the dentist, I pushed the money into the slot, nervously checked and rechecked my windows, eased the car up to the line, and waited.
>
> Powers beyond my control began moving my car forward as if on a conveyor belt. There I was cocooned inside, when a thunderous rush of water, soap and brushes hit my car from all directions. What if I get stuck in here or water crashes in? I thought irrationally. Suddenly the waters ceased. After a blow-dry, my car was propelled into the outside world again, clean and polished.
>
> In the midst of all this, I remembered stormy times in my life when it seemed I was on a conveyor belt, a victim of forces beyond my control. "Car-wash experiences," I now call them."[6]

Have you ever been through a "car-wash experience"? Obviously, we all have endured the "car-wash" at some point in our journey. Often, when we experience a setback we feel out of control. Most of the time, "setbacks" surprise us. We do not plan on them or go looking for them, but they happen. We unexpectedly receive that pink slip from our employer due to downsizing. We get that phone call from a child relating the agony of marital pain that had been not shared before. We receive that unwanted phone call from the doctor with news that we had not planned for or expected.

All of these kinds of experiences and more are setbacks. They can clip our wings. One moment we are soaring and the next we are free falling when we are in the "car-wash" and it seems like the experience will never end. We cannot see outside of the car wash to the outside world.

However, David makes it clear in verses 4-5 that there is an exit on the other side of every car-wash experience. If we cooperate with God, stay open to Him, seek Him and learn what God is trying to teach us, then joy will come at the dawn (at the break of day). He leaves us with our second lesson. *Setbacks do not last!*

Lesson #2 — Setbacks Are Not Final

Notice what David does next in his song to the Lord! He reflects on his experience, his previous successes and then his setback. He goes on to tell us what he learned. He shares another valuable lesson with us.

David's Confession

(vv. 6, 7)

As for me, I said in my prosperity, "I shall never be moved." By your favor, O Lord, you made my mountain stand strong; you hid your face; I was dismayed.

Have you ever noticed that when we are soaring and succeeding, comfortable and coasting, we often develop the mindset that we are in the state or situation we are in by our own strength and ingenuity? We think that we are at the top of the mountain and we will never be moved.

That is how David felt when God favored him. He was anointed as the second king of Israel after Saul died (1 Chronicles 11). Subsequently, God in His mercy and grace made a covenant with David (1 Chronicles 17). He then gave David victory after victory over his enemies (1 Chronicles 18-20). The problem is that in the midst of his success, David lost sight of the foundation of His success. It was not his strength, but God's goodness, blessing and grace that led to his prosperity!

How often have I been guilty of the same boast of self-sufficient security that David made in this verse of Scripture? The word translated "prosperity" in verse 6 describes a sense of "security." It is derived from a Hebrew verb that means to be "tranquil, secure or successful." When circumstances are tranquil, I usually feel secure and successful. My perception is that my own human ingenuity, superior intelligence, extra effort and natural people skills are the reason for the success I am experiencing. When we are "successful," we think that we will never be "moved." We think that the prosperity we are enjoying will last forever. The Hebrew word that David uses in his boast or confession means to "to slip, shake or fall." When he was succeeding, David was convinced that slipping or falling might happen to others but not to him. However, it is only when God delights in us or is pleased with us and gives us His favor that our "mountain stands strong."

There are many passages in the Old and New Testaments that speak to the issue of pride and the effect it can have on our heart and character.[7] In Proverbs 11:2, we read, *"When pride comes, then comes disgrace, but with the humble is wisdom."* Sometimes, God, in His love, will "hide His face" from us so that we will be dismayed. This same thought is uttered by the sons of Korah in Psalm 44:24, *"Why do you hide your face? Why do you forget our affliction and oppression?"* Again, we see this experience described in Psalm 88:13, 14, *"But I, O Lord, cry to you: In the morning my prayer comes before you. O Lord, why do you cast my soul away? Why do you hide your face from me?"*

At times, the Lord may actually "hide His face," at other times, He may allow us to feel or perceive that He has. Either way, the result is one of dismay. This word that David uses in Psalm 30:7 describes, "fear, agitation or alarm." He gives us a vivid picture of the feeling we have all had when we "tremble inwardly" because of life's hits and hardships and realize our desperate need for God. When this happens, we realize that our feeling of "rock solid," self-achieved success and security is an illusion of our own making.

In my experience, the most difficult time to pursue intimacy with God is when we are successful and comfortable-soaring and coasting-in our lives. When God blesses and prospers us, it is easier to seek satisfaction in the blessing and prosperity (the gracious gifts of God) than in God Himself (the giver of the gifts). Was this not Israel's mistake when the Lord delivered her and brought the nation into the promised land? Remember God's warning to Israel the next time you are succeeding, soaring and coasting. Paste this reminder on your refrigerator, bathroom mirror, car dashboard or pillow.

When you have eaten and are satisfied, praise the Lord your God for the good land he has given you. Be careful that you do not forget the Lord your God, failing to observe his commands, his laws and his decrees that I am giving you this day. Otherwise, when you eat and are satisfied, when you build fine houses and settle down, and when your herds and flocks grow large and your silver and gold increase and all you have is multiplied, then your heart will become proud and you will forget the Lord your God, who brought you out of Egypt, out of the land of slavery. He led you through the vast and dreadful desert, that thirsty and water-less land, with its venomous snakes and scorpions. He brought you water out of hard rock. He gave you manna to eat in the desert, something your fathers had never known, to humble and to test you so that in the end it might go well with you. You may say to yourself, "My power and the strength of my hands have produced this wealth for me."[8]

How often we make the "Israel Mistake" of self-congratulation for the success God gives us! When you are blessed with success, always remind yourself of how you got there and turn your prosperity back into prayerful praise to God for His undeserved mercy and favor. Psalm 75:4-7 warns us against the sin of presumptuous self-congratulation, *"I say to the boastful, 'Do not boast,' and to the wicked, 'Do not lift up your horn; do not lift up your horn on high or speak with haughty neck.' For not from the east or from the west and not from the wilderness comes lifting up, but it is God who executes judgment, putting down one and lifting up another."* Our sovereign God is the One who controls the circumstances of life and allows both setbacks and success to come our way. Setbacks make us humble and dependent on God. Setbacks lead us to seek God and sing to God. Setbacks can be a doorway to greater intimacy with God.

I remember the great pride I felt many years ago when my favorite college football team, Texas A&M, was undefeated and ranked second in the nation toward the end of the football season. They defeated their arch-rivals and enjoyed the status of having the number-one ranked defense in the nation. The week following their much celebrated victory over their foe in their rivalry game, they went to on the road to play their last regular game of the season. They ended up getting demolished in a devastating defeat. An article written shortly after the game made the observation that while we worship winning and value success, it is often losing that develops character.

Often, winning hardens our haughty hearts, while experiencing unwanted setbacks softens our soul and makes us more open to the lessons God wants to teach us. Losing can set us free from ourselves and our need to be successful. Valley times can lead us to look to God. When we look to God during a "curve" in the road in life's journey, then His grace can fill our lives. Often, what we initially see as a "reverse of fortune" ends up being the very best thing that could have happened to us because it leads to a deeper relationship with God and greater dependence on His grace. Grace is God doing for us what we could not and cannot do for ourselves. Setbacks are one of the tools God uses to bring us to the end of ourselves and to the threshold of His unlimited grace. This is the third lesson we can glean from David's experience.

Lesson #3 — Setbacks Set Us Free From Ourselves to Depend on God and His Grace

In the next three verses of Psalm 30, David gives us a clear picture of his spiral downward and prayer to God as he experienced the pit rather than the mountain top.

David's Cry

(vv. 8-10)

To you, O Lord, I cry, and to the Lord I plead for mercy: "What profit is there in my death, if I go down to the pit? Will the dust praise you? Will it tell of your faithfulness? Hear, O Lord, and be merciful to me! O Lord, be my helper!"

Notice the result of David's experience! He cries out to God. He pleads for the Lord's mercy in his life. He openly, honestly and earnestly pleads his cause with God. He reflects on the frailty and finiteness of his earthly life. Setbacks can lead to profitable reflection. He realizes that he is absolutely at the mercy of God and asks that his life be spared so that God will be praised and His faithfulness proclaimed by his servant.

King Hezekiah expressed a similar prayer during a time of life-threatening sickness in Isaiah 38:10-20. Setback experiences that "rock our world" can result in greater honesty and genuine intimacy with God. They can cause us to see ourselves for what we are and our life for what it is. They result in new perspective and

144

renewed commitment to what is truly important. The imperfect tense of the Hebrew verbs in these verses could better be translated, "I keep on calling; I keep on crying for mercy."[9]

I think that you can often tell people who have gone through "setbacks." They mark the person. They learn that they are always — forever — constantly — in need of the Lord's mercy and help! Setbacks lead us to seek God and depend on Him! During a setback, we learn to cry out to God for help and we keep crying out to Him for His help, protection or aid.

God has used many books and authors to get my attention, to help me learn and grow in life. One book that helped bring perspective in my life many years ago was Dr. John Maxwell's book entitled *Failing Forward*. Maxwell observes that there is no final failure or ultimate "setback" in life. The only failure is the failure to learn and grow from the setbacks that God allows to come our way.[10]

If we are constantly learning and gleaning from the setbacks we encounter in life, then we are always growing. Setbacks are the stepping stones to authentic success. Life truly is a series of events or experiences in which God wants us to fail forward as we grow into the person He is shaping us to become.

The key to *failing* forward in life is *falling* forward. Setbacks can enable us to fail forward and to fall forward into God's strong arms. Perceived failures are opportunities to rely on His strength! Falling forward, which David does, is the key to tapping into God's grace. As we learn to fall forward into His arms, we become the success God is shaping us to be.

David clearly teaches us in these verses that setbacks can lead to more openness with God and honesty with ourselves. When we become honest and open, we begin to step into intimacy with God. We begin to experience *His strength*, the one essential to soaring and succeeding in life.

Lesson #4 — Setbacks Can Make Us More Honest With Ourselves and God

David's Conclusion

(vv. 11, 12)

You have turned for me my mourning into dancing; you have loosed my sackcloth and clothed me with gladness, that my glory (soul or heart) may sing your praise and not be silent. O Lord my God, I will give thanks to you forever!

The final lesson in this psalm centers on theme of gratitude. The words "to sing praise" and "give thanks" are the same Hebrew words David uses in verse 4 when he calls the congregation to join him in praising and thanking God. The "orchestra" in his heart begins to play as he "raises his hands" in thanksgiving to the Lord. Notice that David breaks out into dancing for joy at the end of this psalm (2 Samuel 6:14). God has delivered him, and he is and will be forever grateful.

When God delivers us from difficulty and disappointment, we recognize His mercy, goodness and grace in a deeper way. His deliverance should lead to the singing of His salvation! It can and should lead to "gladness (glee) and dancing" — great joy!

So often in life, God brings us through a setback, and we are *temporarily grateful*. Are you like me? Have you ever been guilty of temporary gratitude? We are not much different than the lepers described in Luke 17:11-19. Jesus healed ten men who suffered from leprosy. I am sure that each of the men was thrilled and temporarily grateful. However, only one man returned to express his thanks for the deliverance he experienced.

On the way to Jerusalem, he was passing along between Samaria and Galilee. And as he entered a village, he was met by ten lepers

146

who stood at a distance and lifted up their voices, saying, "Jesus, Master, have mercy on us." When he saw them he said to them, "Go and show yourselves to the priests." And as they went, they were cleansed. Then one of them, when he saw that he was healed, turned back, praising God with a loud voice; and he fell on his face at Jesus' feet, giving him thanks. Now he was a Samaritan. Then Jesus answered, "Were not ten cleansed? Where are the nine? Was no one found to return and give praise to God except this foreigner?"

Often when we begin soaring and coasting again, we forget the setback we experienced and move on in life, failing to give God the continual gratitude He deserves. It is easy over time to forget the pain and disappointment of the experience God allowed to come our way. As the details of the experience begin to fade in our memory, our level of gratitude begins to ebb.

I am reminded of the psalmist in Psalm 116:17-19 who purposed to offer the "sacrifice of thanksgiving" to the Lord for the deliverance of God in his life — may it be so with us! It is a discipline to cultivate a continual attitude of gratitude through the ups and downs of life. However, in our lives, gratitude is a sign that we are seeking God. It is also an indication we are humble and dependent on Him. Gratitude is a doorway to God's grace. This is the fifth and final lesson we can glean from this psalm.

Lesson #5 — Setbacks Can Make Us Grateful!

On February 18, 2010, Andrew Joseph Stack flew his single-engine Piper Dakota airplane into a federal government building in Austin, Texas. The Internal Revenue Service field office was located in the four-story building along with other state and federal agencies. After many years of ongoing feuds with the IRS over issues with taxes and debt, Stack decided that he was finished. He evidently had failed or refused to pay taxes and was being audited by the IRS when he decided to teach them a lesson by taking matters into his own hands. He posted a suicide note on his website, set fire to his house, drove to the airport and then flew the plane into the building killing one person and injuring thirteen others. Obviously, years of frustration, conflict and setbacks had taken their toll on Stack.

How we respond to the setbacks that God allows to come our way often determines where and how we end our lives. This story is an extreme example. However, it shows the effect that repeated setbacks can have on us if we allow ourselves to focus on *the valleys* we endure rather than *the fruit* God wants to produce in our lives as we pass through the valleys.

When we pass through setbacks in life's journey, we can choose to stay open to God and seek intimacy with our sovereign Savior, or we can close our heart and become bitter over the "unfair" events that come our way. One path leads to resentment and a granite heart. The other path leads to reflection and a grateful heart.

Closing Challenge

Take a moment before moving on to the next chapter and reflect on the five lessons we can learn from David in Psalm 30 about valleys and mountain tops, the setbacks and successes we experience in life.

- **Lesson One: Even though it may not seem like it, God is with you in setbacks.**

- **Lesson Two: Setbacks may seem like they will last forever; however, set backs are not final.**

- **Lesson Three: Setbacks can set us free from ourselves to depend on God and His grace.**

- **Lesson Four: Setbacks can make us more honest with ourselves and God.**

- **Lesson Five: Setbacks can make us grateful for all God wants to teach us and for the fruit He produces in our lives as a result of our valley experiences.**

Which of the lessons above do you think God wants you to focus on at this time in your life? Are you in the midst of a personal setback or are you currently soaring and succeeding? How can God use your present situation to encourage deeper intimacy with Him?

Chapter 9

HONEY MAKES ME HUNGRY!

OUR NEED
FOR SCRIPTURE (PSALM 19)

William Langewiesche, in his book *Sahara Unveiled*, shares the story of an Algerian by the name of Lag Lag and his companion whose truck broke down while crossing the desert:

> They nearly died of thirst during the three weeks they waited before being rescued. As their bodies dehydrated, they became willing to drink anything in hopes of quenching their terrible thirst. The sun forced them into the shade under the truck, where they dug a shallow trench. Day after day, they lay there. They had food, but did not eat, fearing it would magnify their thirst. Dehydration, not starvation, kills wanderers in the desert, and thirst is the most terrible of all human sufferings.

> Physiologists use Greek-based words to describe stages of human thirst. For example, the Sahara is dipsogenic, meaning "thirst provoking." In Lag Lag's case, they might say he progressed from eudipsia, "ordinary thirst," through bouts of hyperdipsia, meaning "temporary intense thirst," to polydipsia, "sustained excessive thirst." Polydipsia means the kind of thirst that drives one to drink anything.

For word enthusiasts, this is heady stuff. Never-theless, the lexicon has not kept up with technology. I have tried, and cannot, coin a suitable word for the drinking of rusty radiator water. Radiator water is what the two men started into when good drinking water was gone. In order to survive, they were willing to drink, in effect, poison.[1]

In the previous eight chapters, we have been on a "quest" to "quench" our spiritual thirst. We have been talking about pursuing life's most important priority — a personal, intimate, vital relationship with God. Life is filled with its deserts and difficulties. When we encounter difficulty and endure the desert, we often attempt to satisfy the thirst of our soul with substitutes for God. When we do, it is like drinking radiator water. Over time, if we drink enough, it will destroy our spiritual health. Although other things may temporarily satisfy our thirst, in the end they will destroy our desire for God.

Trying to satisfy our spiritual thirst with anything other than God is like drinking spiritual poison. Jesus said, *"Everyone who drinks of this water will be thirsty again, but whoever drinks of the water that I will give him will never be thirsty again. The water that I give him will become in him a spring of water welling up to eternal life"* (John 4:13-14). Here, Jesus was referring to the water of eternal life, which can only be found in a personal relationship with God. Only God can satisfy our soul. He created us for Himself. He desires for you to know Him; to walk with Him; to cultivate a personal, intimate, vital relationship with Him.

To this point, we have been looking at various ways and means God uses to draw us to Himself. God, in His faithful sovereignty, provides us with a variety of experiences designed to create "spiritual thirst." If we desire to "quench" our thirst by seeking God, rather than a substitute for God, then one of His primary tools for doing so is the Bible. In Psalm 19:7-14 we find yet another tool which God has provided for us as we pursue intimacy with our Creator and Savior.

It is important to set some parameters for this chapter before we begin. *First,* this chapter is not an apologetic for the doctrine of inspiration and sufficiency of the Scriptures. *Second,* the goal of this chapter is not to give a comprehensive overview of the purpose of the Bible. *Third,* it is assumed that the Bible is the inspired word of God without error or imperfection in its original documents.

In light of this last assumption I am firmly convinced that the Bible is the final authority for our faith and practice. It tells us how we can have a relationship with God. It shows us the way *to* God and the way to live *for* God. The Bible is our spiritual road map. We cannot accurately know God; what He is like or how we can have a relationship with Him without His written Word. The Bible is foundational and central to all that we do as believers as we pursue a growing relationship with Him.

The first thing that I want you to notice as we begin this study of Psalm 19 is that the Bible is a means to an end, not an end in itself. Although the Bible is foundational and central to the Christian life, it is not the means by which we acquire life. It is God's Word given to us so that we can learn more about Him. It is given to us to that we can more fully and accurately know, understand and walk with Him. It is the primary means by which we hear God speaking to us. It is our "spiritual food" in our journey through life. The Bible is the basis or our foundation for cultivating a personal, intimate, vital relationship with God.

However, knowing the Bible is not the source of eternal life. Christ, our Savior, is the source of eternal life. The Scriptures are given to us so we can know Him more deeply and follow Him more closely. Jesus put it this way when speaking to the Pharisees, or "religious elite," of His day, *"You search (diligently study) the Scriptures because you think that by them you possess eternal life. These are the Scriptures that testify about me, yet you refuse to come to me that*

you may have life" (John 5:39, 40, NIV). John records another statement of Jesus in John 17:3, *"This is eternal life, that they know you, the
only true God, and Jesus Christ whom you have sent."*

In the final eight verses of Psalm 19, we are given several
descriptions of God's Word, the Bible. I want to look at each of
these briefly in this chapter. Notice that we are given: (1) A *portrait*
of God's Word (vv. 7-9); (2) The *price* of God's Word (v. 10); (3) The
purpose of God's Word (vv. 11-13); (4) A *prayer* as we come to God's
Word (v. 14).

The overarching theme of this psalm of David is the theme of
revelation. It is a description of how God reveals Himself to us. We
do not find God; He finds us! We are lost in our sin until God in His
revealing and saving grace comes to our rescue. The first part of
this psalm, verses 1-6, is the story of God's general revelation. It is
the story of His revelation of Himself to us through Creation or His
works.[2] The second part of the psalm, verses 7-14, is the story of
God's special revelation. It is the story of His revelation of Himself
to us through the Scripture or His Word.[3] In verses 1-6, the word
used to describe God is the Hebrew word *El* (the Almighty; or the
Powerful). God is introduced to us in this way by David in verse 1.
In verses 7-14, the word used to describe God is *Yahweh* (the
Covenant God). This is a personal, more intimate description of
God. This description of God is used seven times in the last section
of the psalm.

I trust you have your Bible open and that you will allow God to
speak to your heart about how you can better pursue intimacy with
Him as you read this rich description of God's Word, His special
revelation. Notice that David begins by painting a picture or
portrait of the multi-faceted Scriptures.

A Portrait of God's Word

*The law of the Lord is perfect, reviving the soul; the testimony of
the Lord is sure, making wise the simple; the precepts of the Lord*

are right, rejoicing the heart; the commandment of the Lord is
pure, enlightening the eyes; the fear of the Lord is clean, enduring
forever; the rules of the Lord are true, and righteous altogether
(Psalm 19:7-9).

God's Word revives us

The first truth that David gives us about Scripture is that it
revives us. If we feed our soul in the pastures of Scripture, it is like
satisfying our thirst by drinking out of the cold waters of a mountain stream. We are told clearly in verse 7 that God's law or Torah
is perfect (without blemish; complete; without spot). The word
Torah is a comprehensive term or description for God's revealed
will. His Torah gives us His "instruction" regarding our character
and conduct. His instruction is perfect.

For over thirty years, I have regularly stepped into the pulpit of
the church I was serving at the time and attempted to clearly,
concisely (sometimes), and perfectly proclaim and explain the Bible
passage or topic of the morning for the congregation. Despite my
attempts, enabled by God's wisdom and grace, I have yet to deliver
a "perfect" sermon with no flaw or mistake.

However, the Word of God is perfect, flawless, and without
mistake. God's perfect Word has the capacity to do His perfect
work in our hearts and lives. Therefore, God's Word revives the
soul. The word that David chooses to describe the reviving capacity
of Scripture is the same word used in the Old Testament to describe
the process of repenting. Depending on the context, this Hebrew
term is translated "to turn back" and sometimes, "to rescue,
restore, revive, refresh, or to relieve." It is the same word used in
Psalm 23:3, "The Shepherd's Psalm," where David, the shepherd
says of The Shepherd, *"He restores my soul."*

When you feed your soul in the "green pastures" of God's
Word, it is like sitting down with a great cup of coffee on a cold
snowy day and intimately communing with your spouse. Outside,

snow is falling, the wind is howling and all business has ground to a halt. You know the feeling. You are dead tired from the brutal schedule you have been keeping and the pace at which you have been living life. Your relationship with the one you married has suffered. God gives you the gift of a snow day, and you have the opportunity to catch up, re-connect and renew your relationship with the one you love.

When we take time to renew our relationship with God, much like we would when we reconnect with our spouse, then He restores our soul. He is able to renew us in our inner being — mentally, spiritually and emotionally, as we talk to Him through prayer and listen to His voice through His written Word. When this transaction takes place, God turns you back to Himself. He revives you and redirects you. Suddenly, you are traveling in the right direction again on the road of life. From restored intimacy comes renewed vitality!

God's Word imparts wisdom

David goes on to describe God's Word in verse 7 as *"the testimony of the Lord."* He tells us that it imparts "wisdom" to the simple (those that are easily led astray).[4] The Lord's "testimony" is that part of His Word that describes the Ten Commandments — God's moral precepts.[5] The covenant stipulations or moral boundaries God gives us make us "wise." They are sure (faithful, firm or trustworthy), and you can rely on them. They help us "see" life and our relationships the way God sees them. They teach us to live life the way He designed life to be lived. When we follow His testimony, then it results in our well-being.

Do you ever find yourself being easily influenced by others to go in a wrong direction? Are you ever tempted to travel in a certain direction in your life because the crowd around you is going in that direction? Are you ever haunted by nagging doubt that the direction they want you to go is not the right direction?

If you have ever experienced what I think we all experience and have been haunted by these questions, then I encourage you to feed your mind and heart on God's testimony. Do a study on the word "simple" (those who are "open" or easily influenced) used in this verse of Scripture. This description used in Psalm 19:7 is also used in the book of Proverbs fifteen times.[6] As you do further study in Proverbs, ask God to give you His "wisdom." Ask Him to give you a new set of "eye-glasses" for living.

I recently made a trip to the ophthalmologist. My wife insisted that I go in to have my eyes checked. We have all had the experience of staring at the opposite wall in front of us trying to read the different rows of black letters and numbers. As we squint through the eye glass machine and the technician rotates the various lenses to determine which set of rows we can read more accurately, we often discover that our vision is flawed. We do not see things as clearly as we once did. We need eyeglasses to correct our vision.

It is amazing how a new set of lenses can help us see things more clearly. God's wisdom corrects our spiritual and moral vision. Wisdom is seeing life through God's eyes or from His viewpoint. When we have His wisdom, it is like receiving a new set of eyeglasses. Suddenly, we see life the way God sees it. God's eyesight is sharper than 20/20 vision and is reality.

God's Word brings joy

The third truth we see in verse 8 is that God's "precepts," or divine directions, are "right." His precepts are that part of the Scripture designed to secure obedience or check disobedience.[7] His precepts are straight rather than crooked. They are smooth rather than bumpy. When we follow His precepts, they bring rejoicing to our inner being. Obedience to His divine directions results in true joy. The term "rejoicing" in this verse means "to brighten up, cheer up, or bring joy." Joy is the inner peace and tranquility we experience when we love God with all our heart. When we learn God's "precepts" and follow them, it brings deep peace and great joy to our inner being.

Do you remember when you were a young child and your parents would tell you to do something? Often, we didn't particularly care for the marching orders and directions our parents gave us. If you were like me, then there were times that you decided that you would ignore the "precepts" they gave you.

The temporary pleasure I enjoyed and bliss I experienced as I did "my own thing" often ended in disappointment or disaster. However, when I followed their directions, I experienced an inner satisfaction and peace, knowing I had pleased them and done the right thing.

The joy we receive when we comply with God's precepts is much like the satisfaction we enjoyed when we followed the directions our parents gave us. Our intimate relationship with our Heavenly Father is a child-parent relationship.

God's Word gives clarity

At the end of verse 8, we see that the "commandment" of the Lord is "pure." His commandments are clean or clear, much like the clean, clear flowing waters of a mountain stream. David tells us that God's commandment enlightens or illuminates the eyes.

Hunters will often get an early start in order to catch their prey. Perhaps you have had the experience of being out in a duck blind or the mountains hunting birds or deer. During the dark hours of the early morning, it is difficult to see anything clearly. However, as the day breaks, suddenly things become clear as God's magnificent creation is illuminated around you.

David is teaching us that when we know God's commands we see life with "clarity" rather than "confusion." We are able to walk confidently in the path of His commandments rather than stumbling around in the darkness as we try to find our way through life.

Psalm 119 is another psalm that expounds the wonders of God's Word. Psalm 119:105 says, *"Your word is a lamp to my feet and a light to my path."* Later in this psalm we are told, *"The unfolding of your words gives light; it imparts understanding to the simple."*

Our response should be the same as the psalmist in light of this eye-opening truth. He thirsts to hear God's voice in the Scripture, *"I open my mouth and pant, because I long for your commandments"* (Psalm 119:130, 131). Proverbs 6:23 gives us the same image of God's Word as the psalms, *"For the commandment is a lamp and the teaching a light."*

God's Word brings stability

The next description David gives us of God's Word in verse 9 is that it brings stability to our lives. His "rules," ordinances, or judgments are "true." In other words, they are sure and firm. They are righteous (right) altogether (as a unit). They bring stability to our lives because we can trust them and Him. They can be relied on to tell us the right thing to do in every situation.

Following the Lord's ordinances or rules is a lot like flying an airplane by instruments. Skilled instrument training is a must when flying in fog or at night. Often, a pilot's sensory perception can deceive him during poor visibility conditions. This is especially true when flying over the ocean at dusk or in the dark. The tragic death of John F. Kennedy Jr. on July 16, 1999, in his single engine Piper Saratoga aircraft is a vivid reminder of the importance of instrument training. It is important to know how to read the instrument panel and equally as important to trust the instruments rather than your own perception of reality.

On July 16, 1999, with about 300 hours of flying experience, Kennedy took off from Essex County airport in New Jersey and flew his single-engine plane into a hazy, moonless night. He had turned down an offer by one of his flight instructors to accompany him, saying he "wanted to do it alone."

To reach his destination of Martha's Vineyard, he would have to fly 200 miles — the final phase — over a dark, hazy ocean, and inexperienced pilots can lose sight of the horizon under such conditions.

Unable to see shore lights or other landmarks, Kennedy would have to depend on his instruments, but he had not qualified for a license to fly with instruments only.[8]

Kennedy tragically decided to make the ill-fated trip to Martha's Vineyard that night on his own without the proper instrument training and skill to negotiate the night conditions over the ocean.

Often, we make the same mistake in life. We think we can "go it alone" without the guidance of God's ordinances and "flight rules." The word of God is our instrument panel, which if studied and trusted, will help us make a safe journey and successful landing.

Many times in the Christian life we are forced to fly in fog or at night. Sometimes we are called on to travel during low visibility conditions, and it is hard to get perspective and stay level. God's guiding word brings us stability in those situations if we know what it says and trust the Author. Maybe you are reading this chapter, and you feel like you are flying in a "fog" and in danger of crashing. God's invitation is for you to pursue intimacy with Him through His Word.

Notice that as we become intimately acquainted with God by feeding on His Word, we benefit. According to this section of the psalm, we are revived; we gain wisdom; we receive joy; gain clarity; and we experience stability when we know and heed God's Word. Intimacy leads to vitality.

Not only will intimacy with God through His Word keep you flying level in the right direction, but notice in the next verse the profound value of the Scripture compared to other things that you can buy as you go through life.

The Price of God's Word

More to be desired are they than gold, even much fine gold; sweeter also than honey and drippings of the honeycomb (Psalm 19:10).

I like gold (who doesn't?), but I love honey! Recently my wife was out of town so I took some liberty in the way I kept the house and ate my meals while she was away. Most male Homo sapiens have done the same thing at some point in their lives. During the "relaxed household rules" days that I enjoyed I found myself eating one of my favorite meals in front of the television — honey with toast. You know what it is like. You look down, and to your horror, you have honey dripping down the front of your shirt. It is the kind of ill-mannered behavior my wife has never approved of. However, there is nothing more delicious than ample amounts of pure sweet honey with butter and a little toast. Here David compares God's Word to the sweetness of the drippings of the honeycomb.

According to this verse of Scripture, God's Word, which is, His law, testimony, precepts, commandment and ordinances, is also more valuable than pure gold. In other words, we should desire it more than any other commodity or activity that we can invest in. His Word is compared to one of the most valuable forms of wealth in the ancient world. I recently, discovered an interesting story about John Nelson Wanamaker (July 11, 1838-December 12, 1922).

According to some, his estate at the time of his death was worth 100 million dollars (over a billion dollars today).

Wanamaker was the founder of the modern department store, the inventor of modern advertising and the price tag. He was president of the YMCA movement (1870-1883) and Sunday school superintendent at Bethany Presbyterian for many years.[9]

> Wanamaker, one of the country's greatest merchants, known for his integrity and generosity once said: "I have, of course, made large purchases of property in my lifetime, and the buildings and grounds in which we are now meeting represent a value of approximately twenty million dollars.

> But it was as a boy in the country, at eleven years of age, that I made the biggest purchase. In a little mission Sunday school, I bought from my teacher a small red leather Bible. The Bible cost me $2.75, which I paid in small installments as I saved. That was my greatest treasure and purchase, for that Bible made me what I am today.

> After Wanamaker made that statement, the *New York Herald Tribune* captioned its article, "Later Deals in Millions Called Small Compared With Buying Holy Writ at Eleven."[10]

At Wanamaker's funeral the choir sang, "Jesus, Savior, Pilot Me" and "Nearer My God To Thee." A key passage of Scripture in the funeral service was Hebrews 11:16, chosen by Wanamaker himself for another occasion, *"But now they desire a better country than this, an heavenly; wherefore God is not ashamed to be called their God, for He hath prepared for them a city."*[11] This man's love for the Savior was rooted in his love of the Scripture.

As electronic books became more popular in 2009, my daughter-in-law, Siera, received a Barnes and Noble "Nook" e-book, which she coveted greatly, as a voracious reader. As expensive and valuable as "Nooks" were at that time, the Bible is to be desired more than any other book that you can buy. The benefits of reading it, memorizing it, meditating on it and obeying it are sweeter to your soul than honey to the stomach and gold in your pocket.

The Purpose of God's Word

Moreover, by them is your servant warned; in keeping them there is great reward. Who can discern his errors? Declare me innocent from hidden faults. Keep back your servant also from presumptuous sins; let them not have dominion over me! Then I shall be blameless, and innocent of great transgression (Psalm 19:11-13).

In the last section of this wonderful description of Scripture, David gives us four very practical purposes or effects of God's Word in our lives as we pursue a deeper relationship with the Lord.

God's Word warns us

(v. 11)

Remember when your parents would give you a stern warning or shout a word of caution: "Watch out!"? If you trusted their wisdom and heeded their warning, you benefited. The word for "warn" means "enlighten by caution," to admonish or to teach.

The Word of God warns us and keeps us out of trouble if we are willing to study it and follow it. Heeding the Word of God leads to great reward. The reward David describes is not necessarily monetary or material reward but spiritual, relational and emotional blessing.

How many times have we opened a bottle of medicine or box cleaning detergent and been confronted with a warning label? We know immediately that the contents of the bottle or box are to be used in a very specific way or the contents could be detrimental to our health. In the same way, God's Word warns us, and if we follow its directions then it is good for our health.

God's Word gives understanding

(v. 12)

Are you like me? Do you have any "blind spots"? A "blind spot" is a character area or skill deficiency that you are not always aware of. Unless someone else tells you about it or helps you see it then you do not realize when you come up short.

One of the issues I have dreaded for years is the thinning and loss of my hair as I grow older. It is one of the wonderful "benefits" of not being twenty-one years of age anymore! Each time I make the trip to the barber and he holds the mirror up so I can see the results of his work, I am reminded of the process of losing my hair in the back of my head. The mirror enables me see my growing bald spot, which is also a blind spot.

We all have "hidden" faults. We have hurts, habits and hang ups that are under the radar. We are beset with sinful attitudes, actions and attributes that we do not "see" when left to ourselves. Here David says, *"LORD, help me to discern (understand or perceive) my errors."*

The term, error, describes a mistake. The word David uses can mean to stray or wander or to sin through ignorance. He then prays, *"Make me clean from my hidden, concealed or secret faults."* In effect he is saying, "Clean up my blind spots, Lord."

We can become aware of our "blind spots" if we are open to God's Word and the feedback of others who know us well.

God's Word protects us

(v. 13a)

In the next verse, David asks the Lord to "keep back" (preserve, restrain, or spare) his servant from "presumptuous" (proud, insolent, arrogant) sins. He prays that these "obvious" — out in the open — sins will not have "dominion" or power over him. He doesn't want to be governed or controlled by them.

During the 2010 winter Olympics in Vancouver, we watched two major bobsled crashes. One of the tragic accidents resulted in the death of the bobsled driver — the first ever during official competition of the winter Olympics.

Presumptuous sins are like that. Whether it is anger, worry, laziness, lying, lust, jealousy or some other sin that we are vulnerable to, they can "rule" over us. They are often obvious to all who know us and can result in our "ruin" — a major crash.

The Word of God is like the sides and railing on a bobsled course. The Bible keeps us on the track and on track when we stay within its boundaries.

God's Word cleanses us

(v. 13b)

David's final thought in this section of the psalm is that God can also cleanse us through the instrument of His Word. The Scripture can keep us "blameless" and innocent. The Word used at the end of verse 13 is the same word David used in verse 12 when he prayed, *"Cleanse me of hidden faults."*

We need regular cleansing from hidden faults if we are going to grow in intimacy with God. We also need to be cleansed or made innocent of great transgressions if we want to have a growing, personal relationship with the Lord.

The Bible is God's mirror which enables us to clean up our act and grow in our relationship with Him. The result of acting on what God shows us is rich blessing. James, using this very analogy of a mirror, makes this same point in his epistle in the New Testament.[12]

A Prayer As We Come to God's Word

Let the words of my mouth and the meditation of my heart be acceptable in your sight, O Lord, my rock and my redeemer (Psalm 19:14).

As David closes Psalm 19, notice his heart attitude. In this last verse, we are given the attitude or prayer of a heart that desires intimacy with the Lord as we come to His Word. He prays that both his mouth (his words) and his heart (his meditation) will be acceptable to God. David wants his life to be desirable to God. He desires to be favorable in God's eyes. We find a similar prayer of David at the end of Psalm 139, which we looked at in Chapter 3.

Search me, O God, and know my heart!
Try me and know my thoughts!
And see if there be any grievous way in me,
and lead me in the way everlasting!

David concludes by calling the Lord his "Rock," a term that is used at least 26 times in the Psalms.[13] He also describes God as His "Redeemer," a word used 10 times in the Psalter.[14]

When we pursue a deeper relationship with God by soaking our soul in Scripture and hungering for the honey of the Word, then the Lord becomes our Rock and Redeemer.

Closing Challenge

Our love for God's Word is often an excellent barometer of our love for God. Our hunger for Scripture is an indicator of our desire for intimacy with the Author of Scripture. Our appetite for feeding on God's words often reveals our appetite for communing with God.

Questions to consider

In your pursuit of intimacy with the Savior, ask yourself the following questions before moving on to the next chapter:

- How would you rate your appetite for reading the Bible on a scale of 1-10?

- How would you rate your readiness to put into practice what you read?

- What is your current plan for reading and studying Scripture?

- How much time do you spend soaking in Scripture and letting Scripture soak into you? Are you currently memorizing Scripture and meditating on what you memorize?

Charles Haddon Spurgeon once said, "I would rather lay my soul asoak in half a dozen verses (of the Bible) all day than rinse my hand in several chapters."[15] Martin Luther also observed, "Nothing is more perilous than to be weary of the word of God. Thinking he knows enough, a person begins little by little to despise the word until he has lost Christ and the gospel altogether."[16] The Scripture is the primary means of pursuing a growing relationship with Christ once He is our Savior.

Years ago, I read the following analogy in an illustration book for pastors. It says much about the effect of the Word of God on our lives and our relationship with the Lord:

Consider the difference between a strong and a weak cup of tea. The same ingredients — water and tea — are used for both. The difference is that the strong cup of tea results from the tea leaves' immersion in the water longer, allowing the water more time to get into the tea and the tea into the water. The longer the steeping process, the stronger the cup of tea.

In the same way, the length of time we spend in God's Word determines how deeply we get into it, and it gets into us. Just like the tea, the longer we are in the Word, the "stronger" we become.[17]

I would simply add, and the stronger our relationship with God becomes. Somewhere along the way I clipped and saved this quote. It summarizes much of what I have been trying to describe: "The degree of our spiritual vigor will be in direct proportion to the time we spend in God's Word."

Before turning the page, ask yourself three more questions.

- How much time am I spending in God's Word?

- What is the degree of my spiritual vigor?

- How is my intimacy with God?

Chapter 10

SILENCE IS GOLDEN!

THE STRANGER OF SILENCE (ISAIAH 40:25-31)

I still remember the cold, dark Chicago mornings when I was a student at Wheaton College during the winter of 1973. I will be forever indebted to a short, stocky, disciplined, fiery, and yet compassionate theology professor by the name of Dr. William Lake. His ardent devotion and heart for God is engraved in my memory.

I had just transferred to Wheaton that winter semester from the warm, humid climate of southeast Texas where I had been a student at Texas A&M University. My reason for transferring ... at times I wondered, did I do the right thing? However, I made the journey north to major in Biblical studies and pursue vocational ministry as a calling. I believed God had led me in this direction.

That first winter semester, I would make the trek across the campus from Traber Dormitory to the Academic Building where my theology class was held. Often, the cold winter wind was blowing in my face as I made the walk in the darkness. The reason for the trek was simple. Dr. Lake, much like my drill sergeants in the cadet corps at A&M, was a demanding disciplinarian. One of the assignments for the class was to memorize some key biblical passages from the Old and New Testaments that taught us foundational theological truths.

Despite my mumbling and muttering — thank you, Dr. Lake. Isaiah 40:25-31, the foundational passage for this chapter, is one of those passages I memorized for that class. I have reviewed it often and meditated on it frequently in various situations and circumstances over the years. It has carried me up Hulen Hill in Fort Worth, Texas, during The Cowtown Marathon, when I felt like giving up. The passage has gone with me on cross country trips and encouraged me during times of doubt, fatigue and discouragement.

It is important to remember that the nation of Israel and the city of Jerusalem were in the midst of distressing, desperate times when Isaiah the prophet penned these words at the end of the 8th century B.C. The Northern Kingdom was overrun by the bully kings of Assyria during Isaiah's lifetime in 722 B.C., and in much of the book, the prophet looks down the road into the future to a time when even Jerusalem and the Southern Kingdom would fall into the hands of the Babylonians beginning in 605 B.C. This disaster occurred because of their choice to seek alliances with evil nations rather than to depend on God during times of adversity.[1]

The time that Israel spent in exile, known as the Exilic Period in the nation's history, lasted for seventy years. This period of slavery, or captivity, was not only stressful, but it was a time of silence. Despite the fact that the prophets Jeremiah, Ezekiel and Daniel were serving God and speaking to the nation, it was a season in Israel's life when God seemed to be distant and withdrawn from the people's suffering.

Can you imagine being in exile or captivity for 70 years? Think of what it must have been like. If someone in exile were to describe what their situation felt like in 21st century language they might have said, "The alarm goes off every morning. You wake up, and you are off to your routine of slavery — *for 70 years*. For 70 years you cry out to God hoping for a reprieve or deliverance from your situation. For 70 years there is no apparent response. It is as if God is silent, and you long to hear His voice."

To be silent means to be still or unresponsive. At times, we feel or perceive that God is still and unresponsive to our cries. It seems like He is either unaware of our requests, uninterested in our circumstances or uncaring about our needs. In Isaiah 40:25-31, we are given three great truths on which to feed and anchor our souls during silent times.

The truths we discover in these seven verses, if embraced, can see us through cold, dark, winter mornings and unwanted treks across the college campus into the wind. These truths can also carry us up hills during marathon seasons when we are about to quit. The truths in this great passage can carry us through life and all of its various chapters, if empowered by the Spirit of God.

God's Infinite Power

Isaiah 40:25-26

The psalmist vividly records what the situation in exile felt like for some of those who made the trek into slavery. *"By the waters of Babylon, there we sat down and wept, when we remembered Zion. On the willows there, we hung up our lyres. For there our captors required of us songs, and our tormentors, mirth, saying, 'Sing us one of the songs of Zion!' How shall we sing the Lord's song in a foreign land?"*[2]

There are those times in life when we just feel like sitting down and having a good cry — weeping. There are times when we feel like hanging up our harps. There are times when we want God to speak, and He is silent. We feel like we are in captivity, and there is no end in sight to our situation. There are times when we feel inundated with problems and overrun by the enemy. We long for God to reach down His powerful arm and deliver us, or at least give us answers to our dilemma. Wasn't this Israel's situation?

The words in this passage were likely written as Isaiah looked into the future at Israel's captivity in Babylon. They were dominated by a nation and rulers who did not worship their God. The Babylonians had multiple "gods" linked with the heavenly bodies. Their religion was an astral cult. Idols made by hands. They looked to the stars and bodies in the heavens for direction much like our horoscopes and astrologers of today. It is in this environment Isaiah opens with these words and speaks to Israel.

"To whom then will you compare me, that I should be like him?" says the Holy One. "Lift up your eyes on high and see: who created these? He who brings out their host by number, calling them all by name; by the greatness of his might, and because he is strong in power not one is missing."[3]

During my college days, I obtained the transcript of a message given by David Downing during a training program at Glen Eyrie entitled, "Space Exploration and the Greatness of God." In the article, Downing, who had a keen interest in science and a passion for showing how it proves the existence of God, stated that there are more than 100 billion stars in our galaxy and more than 100 thousand galaxies like ours.[4] Since his article, there has been additional space exploration, improved technologies and additional research. Scientists are now telling us that there could be roughly one trillion galaxies in the universe.

Astronomer Allan Sandage says, "Galaxies are to astronomy what atoms are to physics."[5] There may be 100 billion trillion stars within these galaxies. The universe is so vast that it would take approximately 40 billion light years to cross it.[6] In 1997, scientists at the University of California released a photograph of a massive unseeable star near the center of our Milky Way Galaxy, dubbed the Pistol Star. The photograph taken by the Hubble space telescope reveals a star that is estimated to be 10 million times brighter than the sun.[7] A recent email from a friend contained information about just one of the one trillion galaxies, called the Sombrero Galaxy. According to the article, it is 28 million light years from earth, contains 800 billion suns and is 50,000 light years across.[8]

The Scripture tells us that God, in His infinite power, created the world and upholds the universe with its millions of galaxies.[9] Within the universe and galaxies, God put every star in place, including our sun, the closest star to earth, and gave each of them a name. He not only knows their number; He knows their names. The book of Genesis gives us a poetic description of God's breath-taking handiwork and Psalm 147:4-5 summarizes His infinite power with these words:

He determines the number of the stars;
He gives to all of them their names.
Great is our Lord, and abundant in power;
His understanding is beyond measure.

Despite our new technologies, more powerful telescopes and additional research we cannot fathom the endless infinity of the universe, the incredible number of all the galaxies or the uncount-able sum of all the stars. Is it any wonder that the psalmist declared, *"When I look at your heavens, the work of your fingers, the moon and the stars, which you have set in place, what is man that you are mindful of him, and the son of man that you care for him"* (Psalm 8:3-4)?

When was the last time you visited a planetarium or looked through a telescope? When was the last time you went for a walk and gazed into the heavens at night and tried to count the stars? How often do you "lift up your eyes on high" and gaze at God's creative handiwork? When was the last time you got alone in a park, at a pond or in the pasture and allowed your mind and heart to drink deeply of God?

Every Christmas, I give my wife something special as a token of my love for her. Several times over the years, I have bought her jewelry as a symbol of my devotion. I have given her a variety of different stones in rings and necklaces. Perhaps you have done the same thing for your wife. Remember what it is like on Christmas morning? The tree is surrounded by presents and gifts of all kinds, shapes and sizes. The glitter and lights fill the room as people open their presents. However in the midst of all the gifts when she opens the gift — that diamond or pearl, it sparkles and stands out above all the other gifts on Christmas Day. In the midst of all the other gifts, it is the gift that captures your eye.

Our God is like a brilliant multifaceted diamond amidst all the glitz and glitter of the universe. He created it. He is supreme over it. He stands out. Compare Him to whoever or whatever you want, and you discover that nothing comes close to comparing with God.

That is what Isaiah is telling us in this passage. God is incomparable. God is infinite. God is transcendent. God is above and beyond everything in His creation. He is different. He is distinct. He is set apart. He is "sparkling" in each of His attributes. He is the "Holy One." He is holy loving, holy omnipotent, holy omniscient, holy omnipresent, holy righteous, holy faithful, holy merciful, holy gracious, holy kind and _____ (you fill in the blank with another of His endless attributes).

He is infinitely and immeasurably more beautiful than the most beautiful diamond any human being could ever give their spouse. Nothing and no idol of our own making, not even the stars and heavenly bodies that the Babylonians worshiped and looked to for help and direction, can compare to Him.

Isaiah, after getting a glimpse of God in His greatness, proclaimed, *"Woe is me! For I am lost; for I am a man of unclean lips, and I dwell in the midst of a people of unclean lips; for my eyes have seen the King, the Lord of hosts"* (Isaiah 6:5)!

There is no God like our God, the God that we are called to worship and intimately commune with. John Calvin observed rightly, "Man is formed by God to contemplate the heavens ... for while God formed other animals to look downward for pasture, he made man alone erect and bade him look at what may be regarded as his own habitation."[10]

Man's Finite Perspective

Isaiah 40:27-30

Despite this incredible truth of God's infinite power, we often feel like God does not see our problems, listen to our heartaches, or hear our prayers. It seems as though God is silent. Are you like me? When I go through a season of suffering and seem to stay there, I begin to wonder where God is or if there is a God. This struggle is common to all of us, is it not?

As I was writing this chapter, I noticed that Francis Chan, author of *Crazy Love*, recently preached a sermon on this very subject, titled "When God Doesn't Listen." Often, we assume that this is true because there are no visible or tangible answers to the cries of our heart.

Evidently this was Judah's problem as she endured 70 years of slavery in a foreign land. Can you identify with her complaint? Notice what the people were feeling and asking in verse 27. Then notice God's response in verse 28.

We grow weary and lose perspective

Why do you say, O Jacob,
and speak, O Israel,
"My way is hid from the Lord,
and my right is disregarded by my God"?

Have you not known? Have you not heard?
The Lord is the everlasting God,
the Creator of the ends of the earth.

He does not faint or grow weary,
his understanding is unsearchable.

My heart resonates with Israel's complaint against God. Often, I have thought my way (path) was hidden from His sight and my situation ignored as He tended to the galaxies. Have you ever felt like He was so busy running the universe that He either did not have the time or was unwilling to take the time to concern Himself with your earthly hassles?

There are numerous examples in Scripture of others who have felt the same way. Job certainly wondered where God was in the midst of the devastation and tragedy that knocked on his door.[11] It seemed like God was silent while he suffered. The psalmist struggled with the apparent silence of God when he asked in Psalm 44:23-24, *"Awake! Why are you sleeping, O Lord? Rouse yourself! Do not reject us forever! Why do you hide your face? Why do you forget our affliction and oppression?"*

Habakkuk filed his own complaints with God at the beginning of his book, *"O Lord, how long shall I cry for help, and you will not hear? Or cry to you, "Violence!" and you will not save? Why do you make me see iniquity, and why do you idly look at wrong?"* Later he continues his questions in the midst of his pain, *"Are you not from everlasting, O Lord my God, my Holy One? Why do you idly look at traitors and remain silent when the wicked swallows up the man more righteous than he?"*[12] Jesus, the Son of God, cried out in agony on the cross, *"My God, My God, why have you forsaken me?"*[13] At the very moment when the Son needed the Father the most, it seemed as though God abandoned Him.

There are other examples of God's apparent silence in the Scripture. In the last book of the Old Testament, the book of Malachi, we read this promise from God to His people: *"Behold, I will send you Elijah the prophet before the great and awesome day of the Lord comes. And he will turn the hearts of fathers to their children and the hearts of children to their fathers, lest I come and strike the land with a decree of utter destruction."* After this statement in Malachi 4:5-6 the Old Testament canon was completed and 400 years of silence followed. It was as if God did not speak again for 400 years during the period between the Old and New Testaments.

Again, in the Gospel of John, Martha and Mary sent for Jesus when their brother Lazarus was ill. Jesus delayed two days before coming to their house. It was as if God were silent in response to their request for help. The struggle of fellow servants in the Scripture is often our struggle today, the apparent silence of God, when we desperately seek Him for answers.

Have you ever experienced gray, cloudy days? There are those seasons during the year when you get up in the morning hoping for blue, cloudless skies and pristine, clear visibility only to discover another gray, cloudy, overcast day hovering over you. If you live in the Pacific Northwest in a city like Seattle, then you have experienced more than your share of gray, cloudy, overcast days. According to one source, Seattle is cloudy 226 days a year and partly cloudy an additional 82 days a year. If you live in Seattle, then almost 85 percent of your life is marked by the drizzle of gray, overcast days. As one person said, "The only good thing about Seattle's nonstop moisture is that walking a short distance through a light Seattle drizzle can often feel no more rainy than walking through a thick San Francisco fog."[14] Another source describes the drizzle and gray of Seattle like this:

Needless to say, the combination of low annual sunlight potential and frequent grey and rainy skies makes the Pacific Northwest particularly unsuited for those of us who suffer from some level of seasonal affective disorder or SAD, caused by the low natural ambient light. For example, Seattle's skies are clear for less than nine percent of the time from November through January. We rejoice at even a few hours of bright (using the term loosely) sun that on occasion we are blessed with during these months.[15]

This is the way the people of Israel must have felt while they were in captivity in Babylon. As they grew weary and disheartened, they experienced what I call SAD, or Spiritual Affective Disorder. Much like the physical cousin, seasonal affective disorder, this spiritual relative causes us to lose perspective. We do not feel God, see God, hear God or believe that God is listening to the cries of our heart.

However, the reality is God is above the cloud cover as surely as the sun is above the clouds hovering over Seattle. The Scripture reminds us of reality. The Bible reassures us that *"Jesus Christ is the same yesterday, today and forever."* It also reminds us that God has promised, *"I will never leave you nor forsake you."*[16] As certainly as the stars are still there and God knows them by name, so He knows us by name even if we don't feel Him and cannot see Him. He is still the same all-powerful God that Isaiah described in this passage.

In contrast to us, God is not vulnerable to changing weather conditions or overcast days. He does not faint or grow weary. In fact, the Bible tells us that the same God who has named and numbered the stars of the universe is vitally interested in the daily details and difficulties of our lives. He has every tear we have shed in his bottle, every hair on our head counted, and every day that we will live numbered. We are told in Scripture that not even a sparrow falls to the ground without God noticing.[17]

Isaiah tells us in verse 28 that His understanding of the universe and our lives is *"unsearchable."* This Hebrew word describes God's infinite capacity of understanding to be untraceable. It is so great that we cannot fathom it or understand it.

In their book, *The Hidden Price of Greatness*, Ray Besson and Ranelda M. Hunsicker relate a riveting story about Gladys Aylward, missionary to China over seventy years ago. Her story is depicted in the movie, *The Inn of the Sixth Happiness*, starring Ingrid Bergman. In 1938, the Japanese forces invaded the region of China where Aylward was serving. She led approximately a hundred orphans over the mountains to safety. The authors tell part of the story:

> During Gladys's harrowing journey out of war-torn Yancheng, she grappled with despair as never before. After passing a sleepless night, she faced the morning with no hope of reaching safety. A 13-year-old girl in the group reminded her of their much loved story of Moses and the Israelites crossing the Red Sea. "But I am not Moses," Gladys cried in desperation. "Of course you're not," the girl responded, "but Jehovah is still God!"[18]

God is still God whether we hear Him, see Him or feel Him. He is infinite in power and understanding. He is able to answer and intervene in our lives in His perfect time and way, by whatever means He chooses.

We grow weak and lose power

> *He gives power to the faint, and to him who has no might He increases strength. Even youths shall faint and be weary and young men shall fall exhausted.*

The description Isaiah gives us in verses 29 and 30 is a vivid contrast between the unlimited power and immeasurable understanding of God compared to the limited might and insufficient strength of people. The Hebrew term "exhausted" at the end of verse 29 describes a state of complete exhaustion. It is an apt depiction of those times when we are totally drained of mental, emotional and physical strength. The word describes the experience of "tottering or wavering through weakness of the legs, especially the ankle, and thus to falter or stumble."

One of my favorite movies is *Chariots of Fire*. The life story of Eric Liddell has been a constant inspiration to me. Among others, I often think of two scenes in the movie. First, I remember the scene of one of Liddell's friends running in the steeplechase during the 1924 Olympic games in Germany. Perhaps you recall the image of his friend and teammate as he fell toward the end of the race, tripping over one of the hurdles and falling into the trough of water. He had given his best, a Herculean human effort, to place in the race for the glory of England. Despite his all-out effort, he failed. One of the final scenes of the race shows him utterly exhausted with water and mud covering his uniform as he struggles for the finish line in despair. This is almost a perfect picture of each of us as we run the race of life.

Second, I call to mind the message Eric gave in a chapel service. He passionately and dramatically read from Isaiah 40, the passage we are considering in this chapter. He vividly painted a picture of God, in His immense power and endless strength. Shortly after this scene in the movie, Liddell runs in a 400 meter race, and he is deliberately knocked down and out by one of his competitors. Getting to his feet and climbing back on to the track, he looks to His Lord and dramatically, almost supernaturally, comes from behind to win the race. It was this God and His power that was the source of Liddell's strength as He ran in the 1924 Olympics and served in China as a missionary after his Olympic career.

Our sovereign Lord will, at times, allow us to "hit the wall," be knocked off the course, or trip over a hurdle to get our attention and bring us back into an intimate, vital relationship with Him. As we tumble into the trough in front of us and lift our eyes to the heavens, crying out to the God of the Universe, we tap into His unconditional grace, infinite understanding and unending power.

It is this intimate, vital relationship with the Lord of the Universe that carries us through the seasons of silence and enables us to keep running our race all the way to the finish! The author of Hebrews vividly describes Jesus, our Savior, in Hebrews 12:1-3 as the source of our inspiration and power as we endure the cold winds of life and run our race to the end.

Early in my pastoral career, I read a story about Anthony Collins, one of the most infamous free thinkers in the 1700s. Collins died in 1729. He was the author of the well-known "Discourse on Freethinking." On one occasion he met a poor laborer, a working man, who was on his way to church. The dialogue went something like this:

"Where are you going?" Collins asked mockingly.

"To church, sir." answered the working man.

"Is your God a great god or a little god?" asked Collins in an attempt to confuse the mind of the poor gentleman and intimidate him. However, the common church-goer gave him the perfect answer.

"He is so great, sir, the heaven of heavens cannot contain Him, and so little that He can dwell within my heart."

According to some, Collins later admitted that this simple but sublime answer of an uneducated man had more effect on his mind than all the volumes of argument he had read in favor of religion.[19]

During seasons of silence, which we all experience, it is helpful to review and feed our minds on the truths about God and ourselves that Isaiah so clearly teaches us in verses 25-30 of this passage.

Why not take a moment now and allow these truths to saturate your mind, seep into your emotions and sink into your soul? I am convinced that part of the walk of faith involves fixing our minds on what we know to be true about God and ourselves during silent seasons.

Why Is God Silent?

"WHY, *why is God silent?*" Before we move on to the final foundational truth that Isaiah gives us in verse 31, which can serve as an anchor for our soul during seasons of silence, this question is important to consider. Isn't this the question behind Israel's complaint in verse 27?

I do not understand all the reasons behind the question "WHY?" I do not pretend to have all the answers to this question. Even if I did, it is impossible to answer this question adequately or exhaustively in one brief chapter.

However, five plausible reasons for seasons of silence are: (1) human sin; (2) spiritual attack; (3) divine sovereignty; (4) systemic silence and what I call (5) synthetic silence. Each of these situations or conditions can result in the reality or perception that God is silent.

#1) Human sin

Sin severs our communication and intimacy with God. We discussed this reality in detail in Chapter Three when we examined Psalm 51 and the consequences of David's sin with Bathsheba. The Scripture makes it clear that sin separates us from God both judicially and experientially. Psalm 66:18 states, *"If I had cherished iniquity in my heart, the Lord would not have listened."* The prophet Isaiah offers this same reason for God's silence when he says, *"Behold, the Lord's hand is not shortened, that it cannot save, or his ear dull, that it cannot hear; but your iniquities have made a separation between you and your God, and your sins have hidden his face from you so that He does not hear."*[20]

Often, we feign a desire for intimacy with God; however, we are unwilling to fulfill the conditions necessary for that vital, intimate relationship to take place. We persist in pursuing our own desires rather than God's will. Israel certainly made this mistake. Isaiah graphically described God's solution for their situation in Isaiah 58:3-11 when he called on the people of God to quit *"pursuing their own business"* and start doing God's will.

The way out of silence when sin has severed the communication line in our relationship with the Lord is humble confession, sincere repentance and heartfelt obedience. There are numerous passages in the Bible that give us God's three-step solution to seasons of silence created and sustained by sin.[21]

#2) *Spiritual attack*

Satan, the enemy of God, delights in disrupting our relationship with God. He is the deceiver and destroyer.[22] His mission is to oppose God and all those who desire a relationship with Him. The Apostle Paul discusses the subject of spiritual attack by the enemy and his demons.[23]

The Apostle Peter graphically paints a portrait of Satan's desire to devour and destroy anyone who would follow Christ (1 Peter 5:8-10). His description was based on the pain of personal experience.[24] In the Book of Daniel, we have the description of Daniel earnestly fasting and praying as he sought understanding from God. The messenger that finally came to him made this statement, *"Fear not, Daniel, for from the first day that you set your heart to understand and humbled yourself before God, your words have been heard, and I have come because of your words. The prince of Persia withstood me twenty-one days, but Michael, one of the chief princes, came to help me ..."* (Daniel 10:12, 13).

Clearly, the reality of spiritual attack or warfare is a constant danger. When we experience spiritual turbulence, it can lead to times of silence. These are seasons of spiritual warfare when we do not receive immediate answers from God to the cries of our hearts. The fact that our all-powerful, all-knowing, ever-present God would allow His enemy the ability to delay or disrupt answer to prayer is a supreme mystery I cannot fully explain. I simply affirm the narrative and teaching of Scripture.

However, the good news is God wins the war and does not allow Satan to win the day in his attacks on those who desire a relationship with God. The enemy may win a skirmish or battle, but the war is not his to win. He is already a defeated foe by virtue of Christ's victorious death on the cross and triumphant resurrection.

#3) *Divine sovereignty*

I believe the Scripture clearly demonstrates that there are times of silence that can only be explained by God's sovereign choice. There are those times and seasons when God chooses to withhold His direction, answer or deliverance in our lives in response to our cries and prayers. Sometimes the only adequate explanation for silence is God's sovereign wisdom.

We have already mentioned the example of Job and his horrific season of silent suffering. It is not until the end of the book of Job that God finally breaks the silence and answers Job. The nation of Israel and the suffering of the Jewish people is another example of God's sovereign supervision of human history. We mentioned the agony of the Savior as He hung on the cross.

Paul struggled with God's silence in response to His repeated pleas for deliverance from personal affliction. In the end, no complete reason is given for God's allowance of Paul's affliction. God simply reassures Paul that His grace is sufficient for the affliction he was called to endure. Despite no complete answer for his malady, the apostle confidently proclaimed his faith in God. Paul believed his pain was an opportunity to tap into God's power (2 Corinthians 12:7-10).

Often, God will allow us to go through the suffering of silence to draw us into deeper dependence on His all-sufficient grace. Of course, all "silence" is ultimately experienced because God, in His sovereignty, allows it. Sometimes all the reasons for the silence we experience are known only by Him — the sovereign, all-wise, all-knowing, all-sufficient God who desires us to find our sufficiency in Him.

#4) *Systemic silence*

In some people's lives, there are times or seasons when they may experience silence because of some weakness of temperament, emotional vulnerability, mental disability or familial dysfunction. John Piper discusses these types of conditions and situations in his book, *When the Darkness Will Not Lift*. Piper observes. "Virtually all Bible-saturated physicians of the soul have spoken about long seasons of darkness and desolation." He elaborates and grapples with this issue, "How can we help Christians who seem unable to break out of darkness into the light of joy? Yes, I call them Christians, and thus assume such things happen to genuine believers. It happens because of sin, or because of Satanic assault, or because of distressing circumstances or because of hereditary or other physical causes."[25] Wasn't this William Cowper's condition? Isn't this the struggle described by John Bunyan in *Grace Abounding*?

Sometimes a person may experience long seasons of silence for the systemic reasons detailed by Piper in his helpful book.[26] As I wrote this paragraph, I remembered a recent conversation with a couple at church. The wife had struggled and suffered tremendously with various forms of mental turmoil and emotional anguish over the years. When she would endure a season of darkness, it often affected her spiritually. Although God may have been speaking, she didn't hear His voice as clearly, if at all. This lady's experience could be multiplied exponentially. Haven't we all been there to some degree? Haven't we all experienced what this wonderful woman has patiently endured?

As I stated earlier, I am vulnerable to anxiety and depression, part of my genetic heritage, as well as the choices I have made in my life. When I have toughed my way through "down" times or struggled through seasons of anxiety, it is as if a "cloud" finds its way into my mind and heart that prevents me from seeing the truth of God's unconditional love and abundant grace. During a particularly difficult time of extended darkness several years ago, I distinctly remember a Christian brother telling me that what I was feeling and perceiving was not reality. The reality is, God often is speaking when we think or feel He is not. David proclaimed, *"If I take the wings of the morning and dwell in the uttermost parts of the sea, even there your hand shall lead me. If I say, 'Surely the darkness shall cover me, and the light about me be night,' even the darkness is not dark to you ... How precious to me are your thoughts, O God! How vast is the sum of them! If I would count them, they are more than the sand. I awake, and I am still with you."*[27]

#5) *Synthetic silence*

Often the silence we experience is an illusion of our own making. This leads me to the fifth and final plausible reason for silent seasons in our spiritual journey toward intimacy with God. There are times in our journey with the Lord when we experience *what we feel* is God's silence. These times can be the result of some of the systemic issues mentioned above.

However, they also may simply be the result of our finite human perception, our tendency toward SAD (spiritual affective disorder). Often we pray, we plead, we patiently wait, and we perseveringly plod along during times of drudgery. During these times, we will often say, "God is silent. He isn't answering, even though I am asking. It is like He doesn't hear me or respond to my requests."

The truth is, God's intimate presence, immeasurable power and providential care is just as real during these times; we are just not aware of it. The reality is, God often allows these times to test our faith and develop our faithfulness. Oswald Chambers describes drudgery times as the most difficult of seasons to endure in our walk with the Lord.

> Sometimes it is not difficulty that makes me think God will forsake me, but drudgery. There is no Hill Difficulty to climb, no vision given, nothing wonderful or beautiful, just the commonplace day in and day out — can I hear God's say so, "I will in no wise fail thee. Neither will I in any wise forsake thee" — in these things? There are times when there is no illumination and no thrill, but just the daily round, the common task. Routine is God's way of saving us between our times of inspiration. Do not expect God to always give you thrilling minutes, but learn to live in the domain of drudgery by the power of God.[28]

Perhaps it is our tendency to expect too much from this life and to hold on to our desire for constant excitement, which results in our perception that God has forsaken us. Maybe it is our constant quest for the "thrill of the mountain top" that leads us to believe God is not interested in us. We are often guilty of the "Peter Syndrome" — the desire to build altars and stay on top of the Mount of Transfiguration.

However, the rhythm of earthly life includes valleys along with mountain tops. God is with us through the valleys as well as on the mountaintops in our earthly journey. As stated earlier, it is critical that we camp on the certainties of the Scripture and truths we know about God during these times of "synthetic silence." These are seasons of our own making, illusions of the mind and the result of misleading emotions that deceive us. The silence is not real, but synthetic.

God's Eternal Promise

Isaiah 40:31

Patient waiting leads to personal renewal

> *Even youths shall faint and be weary, and young men shall fall exhausted; but they who wait for the Lord shall renew their strength; they shall mount up with wings like eagles; they shall run and not be weary; they shall walk and not faint.*

Regardless of the source of the silence you may be experiencing, real or imagined, the ultimate solution to the age old question, *"WHY is my way hid from the Lord, and (why) is my right disregarded by my God?"* is found in God's invitation to Israel in Isaiah 40:31. The solution to "seasons of silence" is to persistently and patiently pursue the Lord in and through the silence.

The final solution to "silent times" is to rest in and on God's promise in the midst of the weakness and weariness we experience. In verse 31, God invites each of us — for whom He cares with an eternal everlasting love — to wait on and hope in Him. When the darkness surrounds us and the winds blow against us, God calls us to patiently wait on and look for Him, despite our tendency to lose perspective and power.

God's promise for those who WAIT is RENEWAL of strength for the journey. The Hebrew term used to describe the process of waiting is not the normal word used to describe waiting on or for someone. It describes the process of "the binding or twisting of a cord." The waiting process can often be a painstaking process of binding and twisting. Waiting is not easy. Waiting is only possible with God's help.

Ironically, we can only wait on God and for Him with the strength He gives us as we wait. However, as we assume this posture by faith, God promises to renew our strength. The word used to describe the process of renewal means to "exchange one kind of strength for another." In other words, we exchange our human strength (finite weakness) for God's strength (infinite power). As we experience God's infinite power in place of our finite human strength, we can soar like an eagle against the wind. His strength enables us to run as young men and not be weary. It enables us to steadily walk as an older person and not faint.

Stop to wait

In order *to wait*, we *must stop*. Waiting involves stillness. Ironically, waiting often includes silence. To wait for something or someone, we have to be willing to pause in the midst of our busy pursuits. Implicit in the word "wait" is the idea of taking a break from the stressful activities of everyday life that threaten our soul.

Often, the deafening noise inherent in the pursuits of modern day life drowns out or "silences" the very voice of God which we long to hear. In order to hear God speak, we have to be willing to stop long enough to listen. In order to hear God's "still small voice" — his "whisper" — we must be still!

Richard Foster speaks loudly to this issue in his classic book, *Celebration of Discipline*, as he encourages us to regularly cultivate the discipline of solitude.[29] He argues that inner solitude and inner silence are inseparable. In order for God to break through the silence we complain about we must be silent — waiting on Him and for Him to speak to our soul. The voice of Oswald Chambers calls us to stop in order to wait on and for God in *My Utmost for His Highest*:

> The great enemy to the Lord Jesus Christ in the present day is the conception of practical work that has not come from the New Testament, but from the systems of the world in which endless energy and activities are insisted upon, but no private life with God … We have to get rid of the spirit

of the religious age in which we live. In our Lord's life there was none of the press and rush of tremendous activity that we regard so highly, and the disciple is to be as his Master. The central thing about the kingdom of Jesus Christ is a personal relationship to Himself, not public usefulness to men.[30]

Albert Schweitzer succinctly but profoundly stressed the importance of stopping to wait on and before God when he said, "If your soul has no Sunday, it becomes an orphan."[31]

How much time are you currently spending alone with God? How much time do you spend in prayer … in solitude … in silence … in worship? So often in my own life, when I think God is silent, it is because I am so busy I do not take the time to listen to the very One for whom my aching empty soul yearns.

Closing Challenge

Several months ago, my wife and I had the opportunity to "break away" from the stress and pressure of vocational ministry. I was desperate to get away from the daily grind. We spent several days on the beautiful shore of Lake Superior in northern Minnesota. For days, we inhaled the cool, almost cold, spring air. Our eyes feasted on the beauty of the Minnesota mountains and grandeur of the world's largest freshwater lake.

One day we took a drive back into the mountains and found a small secluded lake in the midst of the tall evergreens and beautiful birch woods. As we stood in the silence, listening to the wind blow through the trees, watching the clear waters of the lake in front of us, my gaze drifted upward. There above me was a bald eagle silently, slowly soaring through the sky, gently but powerfully and majestically circling the lake. As I stood observing his path, the majestic bird spread it wings and slowly circled higher, higher and then higher until he was almost out of sight. He ascended into the brilliant morning clouds until I could barely see him. As I watched the eagle I could hear God whispering, "This is what you need. Stop. Be Still. Rest. Wait ... Wait on ME ... Look to ME ... Come to ME ... Hope in ME."

When we wait on HIM — and seek the ONE our soul needs — He breaks through the silence and renews our inner being. We mount up with wings like eagles, we can run and not be weary, and we can walk and not faint.

IF YOU STAND VERY STILL

If you stand very still in the heart of a wood,
You will hear many wonderful things —
The snap of a twig and the wind in the trees,
And the whir of invisible wings.

If you stand very still in the turmoil of life,
And you WAIT for the voice of the Lord within,
You will be led down the quiet ways of wisdom and peace
In a mad world of chaos and din.

If you stand very still and you hold to your faith,
You will get all the help that you ask;
You will draw from the silence the things that you need:
Hope and Courage and Strength for your task.
Author Unknown

Silence can be agonizing. Silence can be painful. Silence can be lonely. Silence can also be golden. In and through silence, we can learn to wait on God in silence. In the agony of silence, we find the ONE who meets the deepest needs of our soul — *"BE STILL AND KNOW THAT I AM GOD"* — Psalm 46:10.

Why not take some time before turning the page to be still before God? Pull out your journal, a notepad or piece of paper. Spend some time in silence. Read some Scripture. Pray. Ask God for direction. Make a list of some practical action steps you think the Lord wants you to take as a result of reading this chapter. WAIT! Do not turn the page until you have written what He impresses on your heart.

A LISTENER'S PRAYER

God,
Grant me to be
Silent before you —
that I may hear you;

at rest in you —
that you may work in me;
open to you —
that you may enter;

Empty before you —
that you may fill me.
Let me be still
And know you are my God.

Amen.[32]

Chapter 11

Spring, Summer, Autumn, and Winter

THE CHANGING
OF SEASONS (JOB 29)

Seasons come and seasons go
Some filled with joy and others with woe.
Life is a book filled with pages and chapters;
Some filled with aches and others with laughter.
In life's book, we turn a new leaf and open a page;
This is our journey as we travel from youth to old age.

When was the last time you went to your High School Class Reunion? For some, high school graduation is so recent you do not want to go back! For others, high school was followed quickly by the excitement of college, then marriage, and now you are beginning a new career.

Perhaps, for some, the early childhood years are upon you, and you are immersed in the daily grind of faithfully raising (or surviving!) the little ones God has given you. For others, you are single and struggling with loneliness. Others reading this question find themselves in midlife with "empty nest" quickly approaching.

Still others are rapidly traveling toward the "twilight" of life and you are wondering, "Where have all the years gone?"

High school class reunions, meeting friends from years gone by and a walk down the hallways of your old school while glancing at class pictures on the wall are vivid reminders that life is made up of seasons. As there are times in a day and weeks in a month, there are also seasons in a year. As there are seasons in a year, there are also seasons in life — spring, summer, autumn and winter. The writer of Ecclesiastes wrote, *"For everything there is a season, and a time for every matter under heaven."*[1]

Norman Wright in his book, *Seasons of a Marriage*, observed, "Life is a journey which has a beginning and some type of conclusion. Its events follow a basic sequence and progression — sometimes smooth and orderly, other times rough and bumpy. Within this journey are stages or periods which might be called seasons."[2]

In his book *The Seasons of a Man's Life*, Daniel J. Levinson talked about seasons:

> There are qualitatively different seasons, each having its own distinctive character. Every season is different from those that precede or follow it, though it also has much in common with them ... everyone understands the connections between the seasons of the human year and the seasons of the human life cycle ... To speak of seasons is to say that the life course has a certain shape, that it evolves through a series of definable forms. A season is a relatively stable segment of the total cycle. Summer has a character different than that of winter; twilight is different than sunrise.[3]

On the shelves at my office I have a number of other books which talk about various transitions, passages and seasons in life and marriage. On the back cover of one book, *The Four Seasons of Marriage*, the question is asked, "What season of marriage are you in?"[4]

194

As with marriage, so in life. This question penetrates the fog of daily living and helps us focus on where we are in the journey of life.

What Season of Life Are You In?

This is a critical question to ask and answer in our quest for intimacy with God. Understanding the season we are in helps us understand the primary obstacles that compete with or prevent our pursuit of a vital, personal relationship with the Lord, who superintends each season in our lives. It also helps us focus on the common disciplines which enable us to passionately pursue a relationship with God regardless of what stage we are passing through at the moment.

The Reflection of Job

In the book of Job, we find Job reflecting on his own life in chapter 29. Suffering has a way of making us reflect and reminisce. In this chapter, Job offers his summary of his situation as he sees it. The book is the story of Job's disastrous suffering and the subsequent dialogue between himself and three well-meaning but misguided friends. After disaster strikes and Job begins to grieve, there are three major exchanges or cycles of dialogue between Job and his well-intentioned visitors in chapters 4-25. In chapters 29-31 we find Job's "Summary Defense" or his closing argument as he looks at the path of his life. In chapter 29, he looks at the *past*. In chapter 30, Job examines the *present*. In chapter 31, the sufferer speaks of the *future*.

Put yourself in Job's situation and tune into his pain as he reflects on the "good old days" gone by at the beginning of chapter 29. Can't you almost "hear" his audible voice as you read these words in verses 1-12?

And Job again took up his discourse, and said:

"Oh, that I were as in the months of old, as in the days when God watched over me, when his lamp shone upon my head, and by his light I walked through darkness, as I was in my prime, when the friendship of God was upon my tent, when the Almighty was yet with me, when my children were all around me, when my steps were washed with butter, and the rock poured out for me streams of oil! When I went out to the gate of the city, when I prepared my seat in the square, the young men saw me and withdrew, and the aged rose and stood; the princes refrained from talking and laid their hand on their mouth; the voice of the nobles was hushed, and their tongue stuck to the roof of their mouth. When the ear heard, it called me blessed, and when the eye saw, it approved, because I delivered the poor who cried for help, and the fatherless who had none to help him.

Job is obviously reflecting and whimsically reminiscing as he talks about the days gone by ("the months of old") in verse two. In verse four, he describes his life when he was "in his prime." The Hebrew word used here describes "autumn days." Autumn days were days of abundant harvest when the ripened crops were gathered. Autumn days are symbolic and descriptive of prosperity.

During those seasons in life when we are prospering, we feel like we are in our prime. He goes on to describe this season as a time when the "friendship" of God was "upon his tent." The term friendship is the word used in Psalm 25:14 and Proverbs 3:32. This word describes "intimacy; intimate friendship or secret counsel." Job obviously enjoyed an intimate, vital, personal relationship with God during this season in his life.

If you read the remainder of these verses and the end of chapter 29, you notice that Job describes this season he looks back on as a time in his life when he experienced the deep respect of men and abundant blessing of God. In verses 5 and 6, he describes it as a season *"when my children were all around me, when my steps were washed with butter, and the rock poured out for me streams of oil."*

Take time to do your own reading of chapters 29-31. Notice the contrast between chapters 29 and 30. Notice in verses 18 and 19 of chapter 29 that Job thought that the season he described would go on to the end of his life. He fully expected to die in his home having enjoyed the prime of life along with the intimate friendship and abundant blessing of God.

However, as we know from the story and read in chapter 30, life did not continue in this way. God allowed a different chapter in Job's life. One day he woke up and turned an unexpected page that began a new season. Life changed and became very different. Yes! *"Seasons come and seasons go, some filled with joy and others with woe."* However, in each season and through every season, God is constantly calling us to Himself. God uses each season, if we will allow Him, to woo us and draw us into a deeper knowing and a greater level of intimacy with the One for whom we were created. David Roper, pastor and author, in the winter season of his life observes,

> All through our lives God has been drawing us toward His love and away from other affections. The journey begins at birth, continues through adolescence into middle age, and intensifies as we get closer to our eternal home. His wooing is the source of our dissatisfaction on earth and our yearning for that elusive "something more." He is also our satisfaction. When we come to Him, we find a companion who, unlike others, will never forsake us. He is a strong and gentle guide to our destination.[5]

Erik Erickson carefully developed his "Personality Theory" and delineated its stages of development. Daniel Levinson described the "Seasons of a Man's Life." Many years ago, Gail Sheehy wrote the best-seller, *Passages: Predictable Crises Of Adult Life*. William Bridges wrote *Transitions* to help people make sense of life's changes. Dr. Frank and Mary Alice Minirth, along with others, co-authored, *Passages of Marriage*. Bob Buford wrote a best-selling book about midlife entitled *Halftime*.

There have been numerous books written on the characteristics and challenges of the various seasons and stages of life. I am not a research psychologist, sociologist, or professional counselor. I do not pretend to be an authority on this subject. I simply write from personal observation and pastoral experience.

However, in the remaining pages of this chapter, I'd like to offer some thoughts on life's four major seasons. Through each season, God woos us and desires that we pursue Him. My question is, "What are the challenges that compete with or prevent our pursuit of a vital, personal relationship with the Lord in the various stages we pass through?"

Spring

Springtime! There is something about spring that communicates new life. The spring season is exhilarating to all of us; however, this is especially true if you live in a northern or cold weather climate. I've experienced the sizzling heat along the Brazilian Amazon, the humid summers of Nicaragua, and the brutal winters of Boston.

Most of my life has been lived in Colorado or in the Midwest. Winters can be brutal in the mountains and plains. When spring arrives after a particularly hard winter, it is as if life is brand new again. As the snow thaws, the March winds blow, and the April grass greens, the birds begin to sing and my heart begins to soar. In my mind, springtime is symbolic of our early years. Willa Cather, who moved with her family from western Virginia to the plains of Nebraska in 1883 at the age of nine, captures the feeling of spring on the prairie in her first novel, *O Pioneers*.

Prairie Spring

Evening and the flat land,
Rich and sombre and always silent;
The miles of fresh-plowed soil,
Heavy and black, full of strength and harshness;
The growing wheat, the growing weeds,
The toiling horses, the tired men;
The long, empty roads,
Sullen fires of sunset, fading,
The eternal, unresponsive sky.

Against all this, Youth,
Flaming like the wild roses,
Singing like the larks over the plowed fields,
Flashing like a star out of the twilight;
Youth with its insupportable sweetness,
Its fierce necessity,
Its sharp desire,
Singing and singing,
Out of the lips of silence,
Out of the earthy dusk.[6]

As I reflect on the springtime of my life, I remember the cold winters of Colorado and the snow-capped majesty of Pikes Peak breaking into the sunflowers of spring. My mind is filled with the energy of neighborhood baseball and football games in the front yard and sandlot fields, as well as track meets at school. I recall early adolescence in Central America; the excitement of soccer games, first girlfriends, and horseback rides in the nearby rain forest. I remember my teen years in Wichita, Kansas: the energy of basketball games, crushes on the girls I was sure I would marry, golf with my buddies, the physical fatigue of my first jobs and my proud years in the cadet corps at Texas A&M.

If you could talk with my wife, she would have similar memories filled with laughter, energy, danger and excitement from her childhood years in Africa, missionary family furloughs in the U.S., and teen years spent in Brazil.

As you reflect on the spring of your own life, don't you have similar memories? The dates, names, places and events may vary, but the depiction is comparable.

I realize that some reading this have experienced the heartache and heartbreak of the loss of a mother, father, sibling or close friend — perhaps the anguish of abuse, the pain of alcoholism and rejection or economic hardship — during the springtime of your life. However, spring is still symbolic of hope, energy and the future — all of life is in front of you. In the spring, you are not only experiencing the excitement of early life, but the exhilarating dreams of all that lies ahead.

The winds of Spring

Spring, however, is not without its hazards. Just as an unsuspecting hiker can be swept away by a torrential spring flood or a sudden avalanche while excitedly exploring the terrain around him, so we can stumble spiritually in the spring of life in our pursuit of a relationship with God.

This has always been true, regardless of the period we grew up in. There are many potential pitfalls that can keep us from establishing a relationship with the Lord through Christ and prevent us from passionately pursing God in the spring years. The two major obstacles that come to my mind from pastoral observation and personal experience are the (1) *lure of diversion* and (2) *wanderlust for popularity*.

The pitfall of diversion is particularly powerful in our fast paced, warp speed, media-driven and celebrity-centered age. The 21st century is filled with temptations and diversions that were just developing when I was growing up. The diversions I experienced which pulled me away from pursuing a relationship with God can be multiplied exponentially today. Young people today from preschool through the elementary years and into adolescence are bombarded with all kinds of distractions which can keep a person from finding Christ and pursuing God. From morning to evening and into the night, we are bombarded and saturated with a smorgasbord of entertainment opportunities, music downloads, movie choices, sporting events, gaming devices and communication options that can potentially divert us from even thinking about God, much less finding Him.

One of my favorite family events as a young person was going out to eat at the local cafeteria with my grandparents. I always walked away from the line with far more food than I could eat. The endless variety of salads, vegetables, meat dishes and desserts of all kinds was almost overwhelming. The cafeteria experience was exhilarating and alluring to me as a young boy — wow, was it good! In the same way, the diversions of youth, especially today, can overwhelm anyone and obscure the reality of God. Our lives can become so energized by the pursuit of everything the cafeteria line has to offer us that we do not even see the attendants or cashier at the end of the line.

The pursuit of popularity is the other dominating passion of youth, isn't it? The desire for friends can keep us from a relationship with the Friend we need most. I think my experience as a young person was probably typical of most young people. Often, my decisions were driven by the desire to be recognized and applauded by people who I thought were "popular."

Isn't the quest for acceptance with our peers the "mind game" of springtime? Our desire to run with the crowd and be considered a part of the group drives many of our decisions as a young person. This is the other dominant obstacle to a growing intimacy with the Lord that we must battle in our earlier years.

There is nothing inherently evil with the joy of amusement or with the need for acceptance. The Lord provides "everything richly for us to enjoy.'"[7] He wants us to enjoy all the good things and relationships of life. As humans and as Christians, we need love, acceptance and community if we are to survive and thrive spiritually and emotionally. However, as with everything good, the enemy can pervert it and use it to derail us and keep us from a relationship with the Lord.

Summer

Ah! The warmth of summer is invigorating. When spring turns into summer, the activity level of life begins to hum. As a kid, when the school year was over and summer was in full swing, life was never busier and better! Summer is symbolic of our early adult years.

When "school is out" (after graduation), life picks up steam and speed. If you are entering the summer of your life or if you have passed through summer, hasn't that been your experience? The springtime years seem to last forever. The spring season unfolds slowly and moves leisurely, but summertime seems to come rapidly and speed by. How many times have you thought or said to yourself over the years, "I can't believe that summer is already over!"

When looked at through the lens of life, summer can be divided into two parts. There is early summer when we are still traveling as a single person (for some, this phase is extended by God's wisdom and sovereign design). During this phase, we often get married, have children and start raising a family. We find our first out-of-school job, make our first career stop, experience frustration, endure disappointments and taste failure.

In summer, life hits us in the face and gives us a "reality check," much like a hot, humid summer day stops us in our tracks and slows us down. Early summer morphs into what I call the "rest of summer." Summer is that way isn't it? You begin summer vacation and the exhilaration of early summer bursts upon you. You feel like it will go on forever, but before you know it June and July are gone and August is upon you, with September right around the corner.

Norman Wright describes in detail the dynamics of the summer season of life. His primary focus is the context of marriage and family. He titled the chapter in his book "The Season of the Twenties and Thirties."[8]

The pitfalls of Summer

For my wife and me, during our twenties and thirties there were two themes that seemed to dominate our lives as a married couple. These two issues can aggravate our consistent cultivation of a vital and intimate relationship with the Lord: (1) *personal ambition* and (2) *busyness*.

Personal ambition was, and still can be, an "Achilles Heel" for me. By temperament, I am a "driven" person. My nature is to put more emphasis on doing and achieving rather than focusing on being and growing as God's child. I found great help in Gordon MacDonald's contrast between the characteristics of a *driven person* and a *called person*. As I read his analysis and insight in *Ordering Your Private World*, I found myself in the "camp of the driven."[9]

Kent Hughes' book, *Liberating the Ministry from the Success Syndrome*, has also been a tool God used in my life to get my attention and wean me away from the adrenalin addiction of achievement.[10] Both of these books have great value to anyone with this "bent," in my opinion, whether your niche in life is vocational ministry or some other calling. My ambition came from several sources (1) my sinful pride (2) my male makeup (3) my family of origin and (4) my personality type.

As humans, we are all sinful and prone to pursue our "Tower of Babel," which can replace or interfere with the pursuit of God in our lives. However, as men, we tend to find our significance in our occupation. Generally speaking, God has wired men in such a way that significance is a primary need and, as a result, a pursuit.

In addition, accomplishing, achieving and succeeding were themes that were instilled in me as I observed the significant male role models in my life growing up. My "task-oriented," perfectionist temperament solidified my propensity to pursue personal success. I chose a path of personal ambition in my twenties and thirties in the environment of ministry to others.

Maybe you are reading this, and you see yourself in the words I am using to describe myself. If so, you are not alone. Many men in our driven, American culture have fallen into the pitfall of personal ambition for many of the same reasons I did. I pray and hope you choose a different road sooner rather than later.

One thing I can promise you is that if God has called you as His child and placed within you a desire to grow in your relationship with Him, then He will faithfully bring "walls" in your way and problems in your path to redirect you toward the pursuit of Himself!

The second theme that seemed to dominate our lives in our summer years (and still does) was busyness. In vocational ministry, as with most other vocations, it is easy to fall into the "time trap" of being "busy" with business. We were constantly running and going from early morning to late at night juggling ministry responsibilities with family priorities. This is particularly true for the wife and mother at home with children. It is a painful reality if the wife and mother is also pursuing a career outside the home. It is even more poignant for the single parent who is trying to cultivate a career.

My wife was constantly busy during our summer season years of raising a family. She didn't work outside the home, but had constant responsibility for our four children. She was my helpmeet in every way. She encouraged me, stood by me, and ministered in multiple ways within the church to individuals. She was on the go from early morning to after midnight most days. How she survived the summer season years and cultivated her relationship with the Lord is phenomenal to me. I remember someone saying during those years, "Show me a wife with two or more children at home, and I will show you someone who doesn't have any time for daily devotions." Elizabeth had very little "down time" (thankfully, she doesn't need much!). I often complicated the situation with my insensitivity toward her.

During these years, I remember reading James Dobson's verdict on the number one "marriage killer." In his excellent book, *Straight Talk to Men and their Wives*, he shared from his own personal failure and the effect it had on his marriage. Dobson identified overcommitment (often the result of personal ambition) as the primary threat to most marriages. He went on to talk about time pressure and fatigue (often the result of being too busy), which inevitably overtake and overwhelm us because of our tendency to overcommit.[11]

Time pressure and fatigue will undermine the intimacy of any marriage. GUESS WHAT? These same enemies that keep you from pursuing intimacy in marriage will also undermine and destroy your intimacy with God. True intimacy can only be cultivated in a heart of contentment that finds its rest in God.

Autumn

"Fall is finally here!" I love the fall season. I was born in November and grew up among the aspen trees of Colorado. I thought I was in heaven my first fall in New England. The colors were indescribably, incredibly magnificent. I hate heat and love football. When the mornings grow colder, the color of the leaves begins to change and the football tailgate parties begin, then energy flows back into my veins. Autumn can be renewing.

I realize that this isn't true for everyone. We each have our favorite season of the year. In reality, the autumn or "fall season" of life can in many ways be the most challenging of all seasons. Autumn is the season of midlife. Wright describes midlife in this way: "What is middle age? It is a time of life which ranges anywhere from age 35 to the mid-50s. It is also a state of mind; as a person senses the passage of time his values and view of life begin to change. It is a time when he comes face to face with fulfilled and unfulfilled dreams, achievements, goals and relationships. Midlife can be a time when marriages quake and break. During this time, men and women change and so do their relationships."[12]

The "Baby Boomer" generation, of which I am a part, is rapidly growing older. It helps if we are able to laugh at ourselves.

Baby Boom Generation: "Then and Now"

Then: Long hair.
Now: No hair.
Then: Acid Rock.
Now: Acid Reflux.
Then: Moving to California because it's cool.
Now: Moving to California because it's hot.
Then: Watching John Glenn's historic flight with your parents.
Now: Watching John Glenn's historic flight with your kids.
Then: Trying to look like Marlon Brando and Elizabeth Taylor.
Now: Trying not to look like Marlon Brando and Elizabeth Taylor.
Then: Paar.
Now: AARP.[13]

It is therapeutic to have a sense of humor about life as we journey through the seasons. It is also important to understand the dynamics of the fall season of life. Autumn is a time when the leaves of life begin to change, and we realize that summer has faded and spring is a memory.

The swoon of Autumn

My wife and I are currently in the autumn season of life. In many ways, it is a wonderful season. During autumn, the "empty nest" years begin. If you have built your marriage on a solid foundation, then there are great opportunities to deepen intimacy and strengthen your relationship.

The fall season is a time to "catch your breath" temporarily and enjoy a bit of quiet time. It is a season when we can look back with satisfaction and look ahead to future fruitful service. There are benefits to autumn. However, fall can be fatal to your spiritual, emotional and relational health if you ignore the changing leaves. The two biggest barriers I am observing that threaten spiritual well-being and intimacy with God are: (1) the *barrier of boredom* and (2) the *crisis of complacency.*

Boredom — it can be real. By the autumn season of life, most of us have climbed the career ladder to the highest rung we will reach. If you are in late autumn, then chances are you have been settled in a particular "spot" and in a certain role for a number of years. "Been there done that." There is a regularity and routine to life that can lull you to sleep. This regularity and routine can lead to subtle boredom that seeps into the soul. The temptation is to plateau. The subtle slide toward retirement knocks at the door of each heart toward the end of midlife.

For men, this is the season in life when we can look back on some of the mountains we have climbed. It is also the time when we begin to realize that we may have scaled our highest peaks.

My dad used to tell me, "Son, the ante goes up as life goes on!" I also remember him saying in response to a surprise play at the end of a football game, "Who would have thunk it?" I didn't always understand what Dad meant by all his little one-liners, but now that life is moving on, I realize his witticisms contained a lot of wisdom.

The responsibilities of life become greater and the problems become bigger the older we get. Unexpected events take place. Things that we thought would never happen to us become a personal reality — "who would have thunk it?" Our bodies begin to decline in strength. The energy level of spring and summer is slowly seeping from our system. We develop aches and pains. We encounter unexpected crises with our adult children. The responsibilities, routine and painful problems of midlife can lead to the tendency to cocoon. Why not? After all, "we have paid our dues" and deserve it.

The result of the lethargy of boredom can be complacency. This is the second major enemy of those in the autumn years of life. Webster defines complacency as, "Self-satisfaction accompanied by unawareness of actual dangers or deficiencies." Self-satisfaction can lead to unconcern and disengagement. The result of complacency is the tendency to coast.

I firmly believe that God's will is for each of us to continue learning and growing until He takes us home to heaven. The essence of discipleship is the kind of complete devotion to Christ that results in lifelong learning. When we are learning, we are growing. When we are growing, we are changing. Growth and change are the opposite of self-satisfaction and complacency.

There is no middle ground in our pursuit of an intimate, vital relationship with God. We are either passionately pursuing Him, or we are subtly drifting away from Him. This is the subtle danger of the midlife years. Often we feel like we have "grown" in our relationship with Christ. We feel like we have "learned." We see ourselves as "having something to offer others." We perceive that we are on solid ground. However, the solid ground we think we are standing on can turn out to be quicksand that pulls us under spiritually. The challenge of midlife is to continue to challenge ourselves to learn and grow.

Remember David, "a man after God's own heart"? David was probably in midlife, or his autumn years, when he committed adultery, murder, and then orchestrated a careful cover-up of his sin.[14] Was David struggling with boredom? Was he complacent? Had he begun to coast?

Study the lives of the kings of Judah, men like Asa, Jehoshaphat, Joash and Hezekiah. These men were fervent in their seeking of God and service for Him. However, none of them finished well. The tendency to swoon spiritually in the autumn of life is an insidious danger. If we are not careful we can end up stagnating spiritually.

Bobby Clinton and Paul Stanley have done much research and writing in the area of mentoring and leader development. Clinton makes the observation based on his research, "Along the way, there are pitfalls that will waylay a developing leader. Comparative studies of Biblical leaders confirm this. In fact, few leaders finish well! This is confirmed by historical and comparative studies on leaders. Can we do anything about this?" They go on to identify five characteristics common to leaders who finish well.[15] What is true of leaders in the body of Christ is also true of many followers of Christ.

I was an avid runner during the summer season years of my life. For a period of time, I meticulously logged my mileage and enthusiastically ran in weekend road races. Frequently, I ran 10K races with my family faithfully there to cheer me on. One of the things that I learned during those days was that the most difficult stage of the race, for me, was not the start or finish, when the crowd was cheering us on. The most difficult segment of the race for me to push myself, sustain my energy and maintain my pace was the fourth mile in the 6.2 mile race. Every Memorial Day weekend for several years I ran the Andy Payne Memorial Run at Lake Overholser in Oklahoma City. The course was beautiful, winding through the trees along the lake. It was an out and back course, run over an old bridge at the halfway point. Invariably, shortly after the turnaround on the back side of the lake, I would run my slowest mile. I struggled to maintain motivation and keep pace. As we entered the last mile of the race and the end was in sight, my motivation, strength and speed returned as I pushed for the finish.

The autumn season of life is much like the fourth mile of a road race. Often, boredom can creep in, we struggle to maintain motivation and keep pace. If we lose focus and become complacent, we end up coasting instead of passionately pursuing our goal — to know Christ — all the way to the end of the race.[16]

Winter

Burrr — the chill and cold of winter! While spring can be exhilarating, summer invigorating, and fall a season for either renewal or stagnation, winter can be debilitating. The cold of Nebraska is different than the cold of Colorado. The wet snows that stay on the ground often turn to ice, and it is difficult to maintain your footing. The humid winds can be bone-chilling in sub-zero weather.

Winter in parts of the Midwest can be as fierce as winter in Boston where the winds blow in off the ocean and wet snow is dumped on the ground. When the first signs of winter begin to show there is a feeling of ominous apprehension that accompanies the change in weather. Everyone knows the "signs" mean that winter is just around the corner. Winter in northern climates is a season spent indoors. The bone-chilling cold keeps everyone inside, especially on windy days. It gets dark earlier and the sun comes up later — days are shorter. Life slows down and often grinds to a halt. In the winter, you don't travel as fast or get as much done. Sometimes, it is all you can do to get through the day and fall into bed.

The darkness of Winter

Winter is symbolic of old age. In our youth culture, where we worship the beauty of being young and work to avoid the bog of growing old, the "first signs" of growing older can bring feelings of ominous apprehension just like the onset of winter. However, the percentage of people over 65 years of age continues to grow around the world. In Japan and many European countries, almost 20 percent of the population is 65 or older. In the United States, about 13 percent of the population, or almost 40 million people, were over sixty-five in 2009.[17]

The baby boomer generation is growing older. Millions of people are entering the winter season of life. If you are currently in the winter season of life, then you are not alone — join the growing crowd. The average life expectancy of a person living in the United States is now almost 78 years of age, with millions living beyond that. More and more people are living well into their 80s and many into their 90s. If a person was 65 in 2005, then on average, they could expect to live around twenty more years.[18] Modern medicine is making it possible to extend the winter season of life.

Despite increasing longevity and our ability to extend the winter season of people's lives, we still do not have the ability to obliterate all disease or stop death. While early winter (62-69 years) may often be mild and even refreshing, mid-winter (70-75 years) and late winter (76+ years) are often met with many of the issues and struggles that people dread.

In my experience, there are two major issues that can infect your soul and keep you from pursuing the Lord as you journey into and through the winter season: (1) *discouragement* and (2) *displacement*.

As a pastor, I have spent countless hours with older adults through the seasons of my ministerial journey. The first church I served as a young pastor was comprised mainly of people who were old enough to be my grandparents or even great-grandparents. I invested hundreds of hours in homes sitting with grieving widows, at the hospital visiting the sick, or in long-term care facilities listening to people who longed for earlier days. In addition, I have spent many hours over the last few years listening to my father and father-in-law who have endured the suffering and death of their spouses.

The theme of discouragement in the winter of life is real. This is especially true as a person moves from the early winter years into the mid- and late-winter years. It is hard to grow older. It is a challenge to accept the reality of a body that is growing weaker and a mind that is thinking slower. It is difficult to experience pain and endure problems that you never thought you would have to face. The empty loneliness of living without a wife or husband you loved is excruciating.

Apart from the grace of God, the encouragement of others and an eternal perspective, it would be easy to sink into the pond of discouragement and quicksand of despair. As humans, with hearts that long for heaven, it is easy to become discouraged some days even with God's grace, the encouragement of those who love us and the hope Scripture provides us. God did not originally create people to grow old and die. We are "hard-wired" as humans, designed by God to live eternally without the aches, pains, sufferings, and disappointments that result from the fall and our sin.

Discouragement or "down days" will inevitably be a part of the process of passing through the winter season until we graduate into the springtime of all spring times — heaven! When the clouds of discouragement fill the skies of your soul, it is difficult to see God. It is hard to hear God. It is hard to continue on and push through the clouds. It is challenging to pursue an intimate, growing relationship with the God you have loved all of your life.

Displacement is the other enemy of old age. It is difficult to feel like you are on the sidelines watching others play the game that you use to play so well (and maybe even better than those currently playing it!). It is tough to live in a society that seems to value the energy and beauty of youth and disregard the wisdom and character of older people.

This is not a Biblical value. In Scripture, the wisdom and character of older people is to be cherished and honored.[19] We would be better off if we valued what God valued. Sadly, the society we are living in doesn't always see reality the way God sees it. Our world doesn't always embrace, seek after and revere what older people can offer. The harsh reality is that at some point, others end up taking our place without seeking our help or advice.

I have yet to reach this point in my journey. However, it gives me great pain to see so many valuable people with so much to offer being devalued and displaced. I believe even individuals whom God allows to suffer through mental disability are left here for us to honor and love for some important reasons which we may not fully know until we complete our journey. The themes of discouragement and displacement can be seen in the following poignant poem given to me by one of the ladies in a nursing home during my early years in ministry.

LOOK CLOSER — SEE ME

What do you see, nurses, what do you see?
Are you thinking when you are looking at me —
"She is a crabby old woman, not very wise,
Uncertain of habit, with far-away eyes.
Who dribbles her food and makes no reply
When you say in a loud voice — 'I do wish you'd try.'
Who seems not to notice the things that you do,
And forever is losing a stocking or shoe,
Who unresisting or not, lets you do as you will,
With bathing and feeding, the long day to fill."
Is that what you are thinking, Is that what you see?
Then open your eyes, nurse, you're not looking at me!
I'll tell you who I am, as I sit here so still;
As I use at your bidding, as I eat at your will,
I'm a small child of ten with a father and mother,
Brother and sisters, who love one another,
A young girl of 16 with wings on her feet,
Dreaming that soon now a lover she'll meet;
A bride soon 20 — my heart gives a leap,
Remembering the vows that I promise to keep;

At 25 now I have young of my own,
Who need me to build a secure, happy home;
A woman at 30, my young now grow fast;
Bound to each other with ties that should last.

At 40, my young sons have grown and have gone,
But my man's beside me to see I don't mourn,
At 50 once more babies play round my knee,
Again we know children, my loved one and me.
Dark days are upon me, my husband is dead.
I look to the future, I shutter with dread.
For my young are still rearing young of their own,
And I think of the years and the love that I've known.
I'm an old woman now and nature is cruel —
'Tis her jest to make old age look like a fool.
The body it crumbles, grace and vigor depart,
There is now a stone where I once had a heart.

But inside this old body a young girl still dwells,
And now and again my battered heart swells,
I remember the joys, I remember the pain.
And I'm loving and living life over again,
I think of the years all too few — gone too fast,
And accept the stark fact that nothing can last.
So open your eyes, nurses, open and see
Not a crabby old woman, look closer — see Me!

Regardless of how others view you or treat you, do not allow feelings of displacement to eat like a cancer in your soul. It will destroy your desire and undermine your ability to cultivate ongoing intimacy with the Lord.

I am told by those who are in their winter season that a person is free from distractions so you can pursue intimacy with God in a deeper way. Deeper intimacy with your spouse on a spiritual and personal level, as well as with the Lord, are two great advantages of winter.

A recipe for Winter

This is not a book about the seasons of life, but pursuing intimacy with God. This chapter is about pursuing intimacy with God as we pass through the seasons of life. There is so much more that could be written about each season.

However, before closing, I offer this simple recipe of lessons the Lord is teaching me through others' wisdom, my own experiences and his wonderful Word. This recipe can prepare us, equip us and enable us to endure winter with joy as we look forward to eternal spring — Heaven.[20] See if you can find Scripture to support each of these thoughts.

- **Ingredient #1** Be flexible. (Learn to "let go" and give up your right to "control.")

- **Ingredient #2** Accept your circumstances. (Practice contentment with what God has given you and where He has placed you.)

- **Ingredient #3** Focus on being, not doing. (Value who you are, what God is making you and what you will be when He takes you home!)

- **Ingredient #4** Pay attention to your character, not your appearance. (Who we are in Christ is far more important than how we look in the mirror.)

- **Ingredient #5** Continue learning. (Read the Scripture and other good books.)

- **Ingredient #6** Continue to reach out. (Meet with others, serve them and encourage them.)

- **Ingredient #7** Submit to God's sovereignty. (You cannot control winter weather, and in the same way, you cannot control what God allows to enter your life.)

- **Ingredient #8** Cultivate an eternal perspective. (This life is not all there is; it is the "dress rehearsal" for eternity.)[21]

What other "ingredients" can you add to this list? What are some "insights" God has given you to help you prepare for and flourish during the winter of life?[22]

Closing Challenge

David Roper puts life into perspective and helps us prepare for the closing chapter of pursuing intimacy with God with this observation:

> We were put here on earth to know God and for no other reason. If we do not know Him, no matter what else we have done, our lives are a failure. Thus, barrister William Law concludes, "If you have not chosen God, it will make no difference in the end what you have chosen, for you will miss the purpose for which you were formed, and you will have forsaken the only thing that satisfies."[23]

Do you agree with this statement? If so, then what can you do differently right now in order to establish a relationship with God or to know Him more intimately?

Questions to consider

- What season in life do you think you in are at the present time?

- What obstacles are you currently encountering in your pursuit of intimacy with God?

- What books could you read to remind you of the disciplines we need to cultivate in order to grow in intimacy with the Lord? Make a list of books (*Celebration of Discipline* by Richard Foster, *The Pursuit of God* by A. W. Tozer) and develop a plan to read and re-connect with the Lord.

- How can you creatively make the time to cultivate your relationship with the Lord in your current season of life? Consider connecting with a group of close friends to encourage one another in the process.

- Pick another individual you know in a different season of life than you are in. Get together with them for mutual encouragement. What can you do to encourage them to make their relationship with the Lord a priority?

- What one thought from this chapter was most helpful? What action steps can you take in light of this new insight?

Chapter 12

HINDSIGHT IS 20/20

BEGINNING WITH THE END (PSALM 90)

O ur view of the road through the front windshield is always a little fuzzy. However, the view through the rearview mirror is always 20/20.

Several years ago, someone shared this observation with me about life. It is true, isn't it? Most of us are well-meaning creatures who are trying to do the right thing in our lives. However, we become "busy with business." We get caught up in the "rat race" and lose perspective. Lily Tomlin put the "rat race" of this life in perspective when she said, "The trouble with the rat race is that even if you win, you're still a rat."[1]

In the midst of the endless choices and relentless demands of life, things become "fuzzy," and we lose sight of why we are here on earth. The intense stress and pressure of daily living can cause us to forget what God tells us is truly important.

Chasing Hats, Dogs, Bills, and Coffee

For years, I have kept a file in my office entitled "Life's Perspective." It is one among the numerous topical files I keep as a pastor. In the file I have articles, stories, and quotes to help remind me of what is truly important and what is not in light of eternity. In perusing the file, I ran across a variety of newspaper articles. One story from the *Chicago Tribune* describes a 38-year-old man who died while trying to retrieve his windblown hat on the Tri-State Tollway.[2]

Another article tells of a couple who drowned in the Detroit River in a failed attempt to save a dog. Yet, another short newspaper clipping is entitled, "$20 bill chase kills." It contains the tragic story of a young woman killed while chasing a $20 bill across a highway in Cleveland, Tennessee. Finally, there is the story of Rafael Antonio Lozano, a 33-year-old computer programmer from Plano, Texas. In 1997, he embraced his mission in life. His quest in life according to *USAToday.com* is to visit every company-owned Starbucks on the planet. As of October 2005, he had visited 4,918 Starbucks in North America and 213 others around the world. At that time, there were 6,000 Starbucks stores in 37 countries.[3]

It is amazing to me what people are willing to pursue and give their lives to. Yet, are we really any different than the people in these stories? It is easy to get distracted and diverted into pursuing priorities and investing in things that will not matter when we get to the end of this earthly life.

In order to avoid the "fuzzy front windshield syndrome" it is helpful to review Psalm 90 and reflect on the perspective of Moses. This is the only psalm in the Psalter written by Moses. He was uniquely qualified to write this particular Psalm. Moses lived 120 years. He spent the first third of his life in Egypt. He then lived 40 years on the back side of the desert in Midian. Called of God, he then invested 40 years of his life leading Israel out of Egypt, through the waters of the Red Sea and across the wilderness to the edge of the promised land of Canaan.

Moses saw and experienced just about everything a human being can see and experience in a lifetime. He was the only person recorded in the Old Testament with whom God spoke *"mouth-to-*

mouth" and *"face-to-face as with a friend."*[4] He was given a glimpse of God, which no other human being has ever had this side of heaven.[5] Moses cultivated an intimacy with God which few if any have ever experienced.

In this psalm, he tells us the truth about God and life.

The Eternality of God

Psalm 90:1-2

There is no way to adequately describe the beauty, greatness and holiness of God. He is simply the Great I AM. He is the Holy One. In the words of Karl Barth, He is the "Holy Other." There is no one or anything before Him or after Him. He is the One who was, is, and always will be.

Arthur W. Pink in his classic book, *The Attributes of God*, Stephen Charnock in his treatise, *The Existence and Attributes of God*, as well as A.W. Tozer in *The Knowledge of the Holy* have all attempted to capture the characteristics of God. Charnock describes God's eternality and contrasts His "unchangingness" with man's transiency:

> There is no succession in God. God is without succession or chance. It is a quality of eternity; "from everlasting to everlasting he is God," i.e. the same. God doth not only always remain in being, but he always remains the same in that being: "thou art the same" (Psalm 102:27) ... man is not the same at night that he was in the morning; something is expired, and something is added; every day there is a change in his age, a change in his substance ... But God hath his whole being in one and the same point, or moment, of eternity. He receives nothing as an addition to what he was before; he loseth nothing of what he was before; he is always the same excellency and perfection in the same infiniteness as ever. His years do not fail (Heb. 1:12), his years do not

come and go as others do; there is not this day, tomorrow, or yesterday, with him ... "He is what he always was, and he is what he always will be ...."[6]

Moses described God's eternality poetically and more majestically than Charnock or any uninspired writer in Psalm 90:1-2.

Lord, you have been our dwelling place in all generations. Before the mountains were brought forth, or ever you had formed the earth and the world, from everlasting to everlasting you are God.

Notice as Moses describes God, there is no mistake that He was, is and always will be the same. He describes God in the present tense, *"from everlasting to everlasting you are God."* The Hebrew term "everlasting" describes "the vanishing point" beyond our sight and infinitely greater than our minds. God is from vanishing point to vanishing point, and He has always been who He is: *"the same yesterday, today and forever."*[7] Moses tells us that He formed the mountains. He is our omnipotent Creator. He never changes. He is immutable. He is "from all generations."

I challenge you to get the most powerful telescope you can find, and on the clearest night possible look at the heavens. Gaze from one end of the heavens to the other and try to find the outer edges of the universe. God's eternality and stability are beyond the vanishing points!

There is one other truth Moses gives us in these first two verses. Notice that he says that God has been our *"dwelling place"* in all generations (forever). The term "dwelling place" is used 18 other times in the Old Testament. It describes God's dwelling place or His home. However, it also describes our dwelling with God (Psalm 91:9).

It is possible for us to make our home *with* God and *in* God. It is possible for God to be our refuge and dwelling place. The word comes from another Hebrew term that describes the intimate dwelling of a man and woman. It is a description of intimacy. God can be our refuge and home. He is our safe and stable place. He wants to have an intimate, personal, vital, growing relationship with each of us.

This personal relationship is possible because of our Lord Jesus Christ. Jesus is God. Jesus is God's Son. He came to die for our sin so that we could make our home with God. He came to show us what God is really like so that there would be no mistake or misunderstanding. Jesus communicated the heart of God to a world lost in sin.[8]

When my children were small, we would often spend time together before they went to bed at night. My favorite family activity was to read bedtime stories to the kids before we tucked them into bed. There were nights during our early years in Oklahoma City, the tornado alley of the southwest, when we would experience violent thunderstorms and high whistling winds. Our third daughter, Stephanie, and son Christopher were often terrified of the storms that suddenly swept over us. However, at night they were always welcome to climb up into my lap. I became their refuge, their safe place, as we sat there in the living room reading those stories before bedtime.

As with a human parent and child, so with God the Father with His sons and daughters. Isn't it incredible that we have the privilege of an intimate, personal relationship with the Eternal God who created the mountains? We can find our dwelling place in God as we crawl up into His lap (to press the analogy) and seek intimacy with Him.

The Brevity of Life

Psalm 90:3-6

In this magnificent psalm, Moses proceeds to contrast our transient human frailty with our unchanging God, who is our *"Eternal*

Dwelling Place." Notice what he writes in Psalm 90:3-6:

> *You return man to dust*
> *and say, "Return, O children of man!"*
> *For a thousand years in your sight*
> *are but as yesterday when it is past,*
> *or as a watch in the night.*
>
> *You sweep them away as with a flood; they are like a dream,*
> *like grass that is renewed in the morning:*
> *in the morning it flourishes and is renewed;*
> *in the evening it fades and withers.*

According to Dr. Bruce K. Waltke, prolific professor of Old Testament, Moses was the greatest mortician that ever lived. If you do the math there were 1.2 million people in the nation of Israel who left Egypt. They spent 40 years or 14,600 days in the wilderness. The entire first generation which left Egypt died without seeing the Promised Land. This means that on an average, 83 people died per day, 3.5 per hour or one person every 17.5 minutes! Moses had a unique perspective on death. He personally saw more people die and experienced more death than any other human who has ever lived. The words he wrote to describe the brevity of human life were no philosophical treatise; he wrote with authority based on personal observation.

There are many other places in the Bible where our earthly lives are described in a similar way. In Psalm 103:15-16, David says, *"As for man, his days are like grass; he flourishes like a flower of the field; for the wind passes over it, and it is gone, and its place knows it no more."* In Psalm 78:39, we are told that God remembered that the generation which died in the wilderness was *"but flesh, a wind that passes and comes not again."* In James 4:14, we are told that our lives are like *"a mist that appears for a little time and then vanishes."*

Now that I am in the autumn season of life, the words of Moses and the descriptions of human life in these verses are much more poignant. It is amazing how quickly, almost suddenly and without warning, the autumn season of life has arrived. It is like yesterday that I was playing football in the front yard with my neighborhood buddies in Colorado Springs.

It was an instant ago that we innocently came home with my mother after going to a movie to find my father frantically throwing our bags in the station wagon so that we could drive all night to Amarillo, Texas. We did not make it in time, as my grandma died during the night.

It seems like yesterday (even though it has been 38 years) that I was sitting in the chapel at Texas A&M University reading my Bible late one early autumn night in the springtime of my life. News came the next morning that my grandfather passed away suddenly from a heart attack. I would never walk the sidewalks on hot, humid nights with Granddad again after an evening watching the Amarillo Gold Sox.

I never would have thought that my own mother would go home to her "Dwelling Place" a little over a year ago. Where did the fifty-seven years go that I had the privilege of her prayers, loving counsel, and motherly concern? Her last "I love you" will forever echo in my ear.

Who can believe it has been almost than 37 years since the first date with my wife? Has it really been 35 years since we settled in our little New England cottage? Are my two oldest daughters really in their thirties? I find myself looking at pictures of my five grandchildren, and it seems like a moment ago that my own girls were their age.

If you are in my stage of life, then you have your own memories and similar stories to tell. Yes, life is like a dream, the grass of the field, a flourishing but soon-fading flower, the whistling wind or an early morning mist. In Psalm 90:10, Moses observes, *"The years of our life are seventy, or even by reason of strength eighty; yet their span is but toil and trouble; they are soon gone, and we fly away."*

In the summer of 2010, George Steinbrenner, the brash owner of the New York Yankees died at the age of 80. He lived a flamboyant life of fame and fortune. According to AP sportswriter Ronald Blum, Steinbrenner, known for his frequent feuds and clashing with managers, was fond of saying, "Winning is the most important thing in my life, after breathing. Breathing first, winning next."[9]

Is this really what life is all about? When you begin at the end and look back through the rearview mirror in the light of eternity, is this why God put us on this planet?

James Dobson once likened life to a game of Monopoly. I vividly remember through the eyes of a child, the energetic laughter of my grandpa (now gone), my father and uncle as they would gather their properties and store up their monopoly money in an effort to win the game. However, as Dobson said, "When the game is over, it all goes back in the box."

Moses had a real sense of life's transiency. Notice his prayer and perspective in Psalm 90:12.

The Prayer of Moses

Psalm 90:12-17

So teach us to number our days that we may get a heart of wisdom.

On the basis of this verse, Gene Warr of Oklahoma City, Christian businessman, friend, guide and a role model kept a running countdown in his diary of the number of days left until he was 70. When he got to be 70, he started counting up the days he was living by God's grace. As Jim Kennedy, who had an executive discipling ministry across the United States said, "In one sense, he was *counting the days*, but in practice he was *making the days count*."[10] Gene was living life looking through the rearview mirror. He was living *now* in light of *then*. He began and lived with the eternal end in mind.

As I said in the first chapter, wisdom is more than knowledge. Wisdom is insight and understanding. A heart of wisdom is a heart that sees life through God's eyes. A heart of wisdom is a heart that motivates us to value what God values and invest in what God calls us to invest in. Wisdom is the ability to look at now in light of then. God's wisdom gives us 20/20 vision and leads to the passionate pursuit of a relationship with God. A heart of wisdom enables us to put first things first.

On the wall in my office, directly across from my desk hangs a familiar framed plaque given to me by my brother-in-law during my seminary days. The simple words of the first stanza stare at me each morning as I enter and every evening when I exit — a daily reminder of what in the end is of eternal significance.

Only one life, 'twill soon be past;
Only what's done for Christ will last.
And when I am dying, how glad I will be,
That the lamp of my life blazed out for Thee.

If I understand the Scripture accurately, there are very few things that will endure for eternity:

(1) **God** will last forever. He is the Eternal Creator and His Son, our Gracious Savior.

(2) **God's Word**, the Scripture, will last forever (1 Peter 1:24, 25).

(3) **Godliness** has eternal value (1 Timothy 6:6-8 and 1 Timothy 4:8).

(4) **People** (your spouse, children, friends, work associates, neighbors and everyone on planet earth) will live eternally somewhere, either in Heaven with God or Hell, apart from

God. If this is true, then doesn't it make sense to make an investment of our lives in these realities?

The investment of ourselves in what will last forever begins when God pursues and finds us. We do not find God; He finds us and saves us. The reality is God pursued a relationship with us by sending His Son, Jesus Christ to die for us long before we even thought of Him. However, once that personal relationship is established by our acceptance of His grace through faith, then all of life changes. All of life from that moment on should be about our pursuit of God and our investment in what He values.

What Will You Pursue in Life?

What will you chase with your life? Will you chase hats, dogs, bills and coffee? Will you be like the greyhound dogs in the opening chapter frantically chasing "Rocky" the rabbit? Or, will you passionately pursue an intimate, vital, personal relationship with the God who found you and saved you? Will you pursue a life founded on His Word? Will you begin a quest to become like Christ (godliness) which is only possible by grace? Will you invest your life in people for whom Christ died?

Moses is looking down the road to the end of earthly life and beyond in his closing prayer. If you read the remainder of his closing prayer in verses 14-17, you will see he asks God for several things. He asks for mercy in verse 13. He prays for a life bathed in God's steadfast love "in the morning" — in springtime. He longs for all our earthly days (spring, summer, autumn and winter) to be filled with joy and gladness in verse 14. He yearns for God's work and glorious power to be shown to His servants and their children in verse 16. He is thinking far beyond his life to future generations.

Finally, Moses requests that God's favor (grace) be on his people. Rightly so, for without God's grace (favor), we cannot pursue God nor do anything for God. The Christian life is the story of God's grace. Grace is God doing for us what we could not and cannot do for ourselves. Without His favor, the journey is in vain. Moses requests God's favor so that "the work of our hands," the investment made with their lives, would be "established" or "confirmed."

This final thought is his heartfelt yearning for the work and pursuit of their lives "to stand" or be "set." It was his passionate desire that what he pursued with his life last for eternity.

It Begins and Ends with God

It has been the thesis of this book that a life invested in life's priorities, the eternal realities that matter in the end, begins with the pursuit of life's first priority, an intimate, personal, vital relationship with the God who made us and saved us (Matthew 22:37). The journey God takes us on to rid us of our desire for other things so that we desire the One thing that will satisfy our desires is a lifelong process. The journey begins with the Savior, spirals through all the seasons of life, and includes all of the tools and processes discussed in the preceding pages. David Roper quotes Augustine and summarizes in a few sentences what I have been trying to say in an entire book!

> The happiness we are seeking in all our "getting" is truly found only in loving and being loved by God ... In His love we find full satisfaction.

> Indeed, all our wanting and getting is nothing more than a symptom of the heart's deepest desire — the desire for God Himself. We were made to be filled and flooded with God alone; there is thus an infinite space within us that no number of toys or other joys can fill. Only infinite Love will do.

God is not just one more good thing among others. He is the cause of all good, the "giver of every good and perfect gift" — the source of "the good life" and the happiness we seek.

"One who has God has everything," Augustine wrote. "And one who has everything except God has nothing."[11]

Closing Challenge

To begin with the end in mind requires reflection. To look at *now* in light of *then* and begin the passionate pursuit of a deeper relationship with the Lord who created you, loved you, died for you, pursued you, found you and saved you demands intentionality. Pursuing an intimate relationship with God will not happen by accident.

What can you take away from Moses' psalm and apply to your life? What one or two thoughts from Psalm 90 will help you in your continued quest for greater intimacy with God? Who can you link up with for encouragement in your journey toward knowing Christ more deeply?

Do not close this book without jotting down your closing thoughts. Every journey begins with a first step. With the amazing grace of God, no matter what your past may be, it is never too late to begin pursuing intimacy with the God who loves you.

Those Wasted Years

I looked upon a farm one day,
That I used to own;
The barn had fallen to the ground,
The fields were overgrown.

The house in which my children grew,
Where we had lived for years —
I turned to see it broken down,
And brushed aside the tears.

I looked upon my soul one day,
To find it too had grown
With thorns and nettles everywhere,
The seeds neglect had sown.

The years had passed while I had cared
For things of lesser worth:
The things of Heaven I let go
When minding things of Earth.

To Christ I turned with bitter tears,
And cried, O Lord, forgive!
I haven't much time left for Thee,
Not many years to live."

The wasted years forever gone,
The days I can't recall;
If I could live those days again,
I'd make Him Lord of all.[12]
— *Theodore W. Brennan*

The good news of God's glorious, gracious gospel is that no matter how many days, weeks, months or years it has been, you can still begin again in your pursuit to know Christ more deeply and love God more fully. He is waiting for you to begin the quest for intimacy with Himself.

ENDNOTES

Preface
1 Simon Tugwell, *The Beatitudes: Soundings in Christian Traditions* (Springfield, IL: Templegate, 1980), 76.
2 Augustine, ed. Philip Schaff, trans. J. G. Pilkington, *The Confessions and Letters of St. Augustine, vol. 1, A Select Library of the Nicene and Post-Nicene Fathers of the Christian Church* (Grand Rapids: Wm. B. Eerdmans, 1974), 1.
3 A. W. Tozer, *The Pursuit of God* (Harrisburg, PA: Christian Publications, 1948), 11-12.
4 C. S. Lewis, *Mere Christianity* (New York: HarperSanFrancisco, 2001), 136-137.

Chapter One
1 Ephesians 5:15 (NIV).
2 Proverbs 1:8-9 and Proverbs 1:20-21.
3 Diogenes Laertius, trans. Robert Drew Hicks, *Lives of Eminent Philosophers, vol. 1, The Loeb Classical Library* (Cambridge, MA: Harvard University Press, 1966), 91.
4 David Dunning delineates this issue at length and cites Thales in his excellent book *Self-Insight: Roadblocks and Detours on the Path to Knowing Thyself* (New York: Psychology Press, 2005), 3.
5 Please note the following sources for more reading or research on this issue: David Benner, *The Gift of Being Yourself: The Sacred Call to Self-Discovery* (Downers Grove, IL: InterVarsity, 2004), bk.; Daniel Goleman and Annie McKee, *Primal Leadership: Learning to Lead with Emotional Intelligence* (Boston: Harvard Business School Press, 2004), bk.; Manuel London, *Leadership Development: Paths to Self-Insight and Professional Growth* (Mahwah, NJ: Lawrence Erlbaum Associates, 2002), bk.; Cynthia D. McCauley and Ellen Van Velsor, eds., *The Center for Creative Leadership Handbook of Leadership Development* (San Francisco: Jossey-Bass, 2004), bk.; Thomas Merton, *New Seeds of Contemplation* (New York: New Directions, 1961), bk.
6 Sherwood Eliot Wirt and Kersten Beckstrom, eds., *Topical Encyclopedia of Living Quotations* (Minneapolis: Bethany House, 1982), 255.
7 For further reading on the importance of character in leader development, please note the following books for a few examples: Warren Bennis, *On Becoming a Leader* (Reading, MA: Addison-Wesley, 1989), bk.; Tom Osborne, *Faith In The Game* (Colorado Springs, CO: WaterBrook Press, 1999), 1-14; Bill Thrall, Bruce McNicol, and Ken McElrath, *The Ascent of a Leader* (San Francisco: Jossey-Bass, 1999), 1- 2, 31-34; Carson Pue, *Mentoring Leaders: Wisdom for Developing Character, Calling, and Competency* (Grand Rapids: Baker Books, 2005), bk.
8 Bob Kelly, *Worth Repeating: More Than 5,000 Classic and Contemporary Quotes* (Grand Rapids: Kregel Publications, 2003), 41.
9 Stephen Covey, *The Seven Habits of Highly Effective People* (New York: Fireside Simon & Schuster Press, 1989), 97-98.
10 J. I. Packer, *Knowing God* (Downers Grove, IL: InterVarsity Press, 1973), 5-6.
11 Ibid., 21.
12 Tim Sanders, www.sanderssays.typepad.com, August 25, 2006, submitted by Gino Grunberg, Gig Harbor, WA in PreachingToday.com.

Chapter Two
1 Paul Lee Tan, *Encyclopedia of 7700 Illustrations: Signs of the Times* (Rockville, MD: Assurance Publishers, 1979), 1039.
2 Augustine, Schaff, and Pilkington, *Confessions and Letters of St. Augustine*, 1:1.
3 For a good overview of both the biblical basis for and historical background of Solemn Assemblies, one can read this eleven page study by the Presbyterian Church USA entitled "Biblical and Historical Background on Solemn Assemblies," March 16, 2010, 1-11, found at http://www.pcusa.org/media/uploads/theologyandworship /pdfs/biblicalhistoricalbackground.pdf (accessed July 2010).
4 Tozer, *Pursuit of God*, 69-70.
5 A. W. Tozer, *That Incredible Christian* (Harrisburg, PA: Christian Publications, 1964), 46.
6 ESV Study Bible (Wheaton, IL: Crossway Bibles, 2008), 1650 (study note).
7 David Mordkoff, "American Emmons Misses Out on Gold by Firing at Wrong Target," www.Sports.Yahoo.com, August 22, 2004, submitted by Alan Price, Chatsworth, GA in PreachingToday.com.

Chapter Three
1 Sharon Begley, "The Roots of Evil," *Newsweek*, May 21, 2001, 31-32, submitted by Jeffrey D. Arthurs, Portland, OR in PreachingToday.com.
2 The source for this particular rendition of the story told by Dr. H. A. Ironside is unknown. For another version of the story please note the tract by Oswald J. Smith, *Who Can Pay So Much?* (Willowdale, Ontario, Canada: The People's Church, Toronto). The printed version of this tract is now permanently stored in the Billy Graham Center Museum in Wheaton, Illinois.
3 Mark Water, *New Encyclopedia of Christian Quotations* (Grand Rapids: Baker Books, 2000), 377. Augustine argues this theological tenet of human depravity at length in his Anti-Pelagian writings. This can be seen especially in his treatise on "The Grace of Christ and on Orginal Sin" and his treatise on "Grace and Free Will." These treatises can be found in Augustine, ed. Philip Schaff, *St. Augustine: Anti-Pelagian Writings, first series, vol. 5, Select library of the Nicene and post-Nicene fathers* (Grand Rapids: Eerdmans, 1971).
4 For a brief explanation of the background to this imagery David uses in Psalm 51:7, please see the study notes in Kenneth L. Barker and Donald W. Burdick, eds., Zondervan NIV Study Bible: New International Version (Grand Rapids: Zondervan, 2002), 164, 843.
5 For two good overviews of this doctrinal distinction between the testaments please note John R. W. Stott, *The Baptism and Fullness of the Holy Spirit* (Downers Grove, IL: Inter-Varsity Press, 1975), bk.; and Billy Graham, *The Holy Spirit: Activating God's Power in Your Life* (Waco, TX: Word Books, 1978), bk.
6 Frank E. Gaebelein, *The Expositor's Bible Commentary: With the New International Version* (Grand Rapids: Zondervan, 1991), 5:382.

Chapter Four
1 Martha Snell Nicholson, "Treasures," in *Ivory Palaces* (Chicago: Moody Press, 1949), 67. Martha Snell Nicholson was a woman who suffered from four incurable diseases. She struggled with pain more than thirty-five years, an invalid, bound to her bed.
2 Henry G. Bosch, "How God Makes Comforters," *Our Daily Bread* (Grand Rapids: RBC Ministries, 1993). Used by permission. All rights reserved.
3 This beautiful poem can be found in V. Raymond Edman, *The Disciplines of Life: Choosing Growth in Every Circumstance* (Wheaton, IL: Scripture Press Foundation, 1948), 196.

Chapter Five
1 "Survey: Christians Worldwide Too Busy For God," www.christian post.com, submitted by Van Morris, Mount Washington, KY in Preaching Today.com.
2 http://www.welshrevival.com/lang-en/1904history.htm (accessed July 2010).
3 Jonah 2:8 (NIV).
4 For resources dealing with depression, please note Jeff Olson, *When Hope Is Lost: Dealing with Depression, Discovery Series* (Grand Rapids: RBC Ministries, 2002), bk.; Frank B. Minirth and Paul D. Meier, *Happiness Is a Choice: A Manual on the Symptoms, Causes and Cures of Depression* (Grand Rapids: Baker Book House, 1988), bk.; and Stephen Arterburn, *Hand-Me-Down Genes and Second-Hand Emotions* (Nashville: Oliver Nelson, 1992), bk. For resources on anxiety, please note John Haggai, *How To Win Over Fear* (Eugene, OR: Harvest House, 1987), bk.; William Backus, *The Good News About Worry* (Minneapolis: Bethany House, 1991), bk.; Norman H. Wright, *Afraid No More!* (Wheaton, IL: Tyndale House, 1992), bk.; and *What Can I Do With My Worry? Discovery Series* (Grand Rapids: RBC Ministries, 1992), bk.
5 Kenneth W. Osbeck, *101 Hymn Stories* (Grand Rapids: Kregel Publications, 1982), 264-265; Kenneth W. Osbeck, *101 More Hymn Stories* (Grand Rapids: Kregel Publications, 1985), 208-209; Michael E. Rusten and Sharon O. Rusten, *The One Year Book of Christian History* (Wheaton, IL: Tyndale House, 2003), 140-141.
6 For obvious and frequent examples of this, one can read John Bunyan, *The Pilgrim's Progress, The Christian Library* (Uhrichsville, OH: Barbour), bk.; and John Bunyan, *Grace Abounding To The Chief Of Sinners* (New York: Cosimo, 2007), bk.
7 Kent R. Hughes and Barbara Hughes, *Liberating Ministry from the Success Syndrome* (Wheaton, IL: Tyndale House, 1987), 143.
8 Ibid.
9 John Piper, "Charles Spurgeon: preaching through adversity," *Founders Journal*, no. 23 (Winter 1996): 5-21, quoted in Leith Anderson, *Leadership that Works* (Minneapolis: Bethany House, 1999), 175.
10 Joanie Yoder, *The God-Dependent Life* (London: Hodder & Stoughton, 1991), bk.; Joanie Yoder, *God Alone: Heartfelt Encouragement from the Pages of Our Daily Bread* (Grand Rapids: Discovery House, 2006), bk.
11 Beth Moore, *Get Out of That Pit: Straight Talk about God's Deliverance from a Former Pit-Dweller* (Nashville: Integrity Publishers, 2007), bk.
12 Arthur E. Jongsma Jr., "Depression," Banner (OK), n.d.
13 C. H. Spurgeon, *The Treasury of David: Containing an Original Exposition of the Book of Psalms; a Collection of Illustrative Extracts from the Whole Range of Literature; a Series of Homiletical Hints Upon Almost Every Verse; and Lists of Writers Upon Each Psalm* (McLean, VA: MacDonald, 1987), 1:273.
14 Ibid., 272.
15 Donald Guthrie, J. A. Motyer, and Francis Davidson, *The New Bible Commentary: Revised* (Grand Rapids: Eerdmans, 1970), 478.
16 Tan, *Encyclopedia of 7700 Illustrations*, 754-755.
17 Author unknown.

Chapter Six
1 National Center for Case Study Teaching in Science, 1999-2010, http://www.sciences.org/thermoregulation/thermoregulation.asp (accessed July 2010).
2 H. D. McCarty, "Overcoming the Hard Hits of Life," *Mandate For Men* (Fayetteville, AR: Ventures For Christ, December 1993), 2.

3 Mike Yaconelli, *Messy Spirituality: God's Annoying Love for Imperfect People* (Grand Rapids: Zondervan, 2002), 13.
4 This poem is from Dr. Paul B. Long, retired professor from Reformed Theological Seminary in Clinton, Mississippi. Dr. Long was a missionary church planter in Africa and Brazil. He also served in the armed services in Burma during World War II.

Chapter Seven
1 Tan, *Encyclopedia of 7700 Illustrations*, 763.
2 The source for the exact wording of this quote is unknown. For a similar wording of the quotation please see Frank E. Gaebelein, *The Expositor's Bible Commentary: With the New International Version* (Grand Rapids: Zondervan, 1981), 12:434.
3 Gordon MacDonald, *Ordering Your Private World* (Nashville: Thomas Nelson, 1985), 164.
4 I would consider activities such as excessive surfing of the Internet, hours of television or movies, facebooking, blogging, texting, and constant connection via cell phone as examples of "technology overload."
5 Richard J. Foster, *Celebration of Discipline* (San Francisco: Harper & Row, 1978), bk.; Donald S. Whitney, *Spiritual Disciplines for the Christian Life* (Colorado Springs, CO: NavPress, 1991), bk.

Chapter Eight
1 John Piper, *A Sweet and Bitter Providence: Sex, Race, and the Sovereignty of God.* (Wheaton, IL: Crossway Books, 2010), 101-102.
2 Spurgeon, *Treasury of David*, 1:43.
3 Please note Psalm 6:2, 41:4, 60:2, 103:3, 107:20, and 147:3 for further references where this image and word are used.
4 Tan, *Encyclopedia of 7700 Illustrations*, 1648.
5 Mrs. Charles E. Cowman and James Reimann, *Streams in the Desert: 366 Daily Devotional Readings* (Grand Rapids: Zondervan, 1997), 313.
6 Joanie Yoder, "In The Car Wash," *Our Daily Bread* (Grand Rapids: RBC Ministries, 2010), February 17, 2010. Used by permission. All rights reserved.
7 Note the warnings in Proverbs 6:17, 16:18, 18:12, 21:4, 29:23 and 1 Corinthians 10:12 and the following references on the danger of pride in our lives: Obadiah 1:2-4; Mark 7:21-23; 1 Timothy 6:17; James 4:6; and 1 Peter 5:5.
8 Deuteronomy 8:10-18 (NIV).
9 Gaebelein, *Expositor's Bible Commentary*, 5:261.
10 John C. Maxwell, *Failing Forward: Turning Mistakes into Stepping-Stones for Success* (Nashville: Thomas Nelson, 2000), bk.

Chapter Nine
1 William Langewiesche, *Sahara Unveiled: A Journey Across the Desert* (New York: Vintage Books, 1997), submitted by Jeff Ingram in PreachingToday.com.
2 Please note Romans 1:19-25 for another example and further teaching on God's general revelation of Himself through creation.
3 Please note passages such as Psalm 119; 2 Timothy 3:15-17; 2 Peter 1:16-21; and Hebrews 1:1-2 for further teaching on God's special revelation of Himself through the Scripture.
4 Franz Delitzsch and Carl Friedrich Keil, *Psalms* (Peabody, MA: Hendrickson, 1996), 179.
5 Study the following verses as cross references: Exodus 16:34, 25:16, 31:18 and Deuteronomy 9:9.

6 Proverbs 14:15 and Proverbs 22:3 are two examples of where this description is used.

7 W. Graham Scroggie, *The Psalms: Psalms I to CL* (Old Tappan, NJ: Fleming H. Revell, 1978), 125.

8 http://www.history.com/this-day-in-history/jfk-jr-killed-in-plane-crash (accessed July 2010).

9 http://www.answers.com/topic/john-wanamaker (accessed July 2010).

10 Tan, *Encyclopedia of 7700 Illustrations*, 190.

11 "WANAMAKER BURIED WITH HIGH TRIBUTES; Mayors Hylan and Moore and Other Officials Attend Philadelphia Services. THOUSANDS AT THE CHURCH. Honors Paid as Cortege Passes—Stores and Schools Suspend—Flowers From Employees," Special to the *New York Times*, December 15, 1922.

12 James 1:23-25.

13 Psalm 18:2, 31, 46 and Psalm 62:2, 6, 7 are some other places where the word is used.

14 Note Psalm 103:4 and Psalm 107:2 for some instances of the use of this word.

15 C. H. Spurgeon, "Sayings of Spurgeon: A sampling of his wisdom and wit," compiled by Mary Ann Jeffreys, *Christian History 29* (January 1991). For a more complete version of this quote please see: *C. H. Spurgeon, The Metropolitan Tabernacle Pulpit: Sermons Preached and Revised by C.H. Spurgeon, During the Year 1871* (London: Passmore & Alabaster, 1872) Sermon 1578, 42.

16 Martin Luther, *Commentary on the Epistle to the Galatians*, trans. Theodore Graebner (Grand Rapids: Zondervan, 1949), http://www.ntslibrary.com /PDF Books/Luther Commentary on Galatians.pdf, 19.

17 Michael P. Green, *Illustrations for Biblical Preaching* (Grand Rapids: Baker Book House, 1989), 31.

Chapter Ten

1 Note Isaiah chapters 7, 36 and 37 for background to this passage and the setting of the book.

2 Psalm 137:1-4.

3 Isaiah 40:25-26 (RSV).

4 David W. Downing, "Space Exploration and the Greatness of God" (transcript, Glen Eyrie *Training Program*, The Navigators, Summer 1970).

5 Neil McAleer, *The Mind-Boggling Universe* (Garden City, NY: Doubleday, 1987), quoted in Craig B. Larson, *Choice Contemporary Stories and Illustrations* (Grand Rapids: Baker Books, 1998), 54.

6 Ibid.

7 George Johnson, "Casting an Eye on Sights Unseen," *New York Times*, October 12, 1997, quoted in Craig B. Larson, *Choice Contemporary Stories and Illustrations* (Grand Rapids: Baker Books, 1998), 261.

8 The source of this information and accompanying photographs can be found at http://www.dailymail.co.uk/legacygallery-9139/Hubble and http://hubblesite.org (accessed July 2010).

9 Hebrews 1:1-3.

10 John Calvin, *Commentaii in Isaiam prophetam* (Geneva, 1570. E. T. Grand Rapids, 1850), quoted in Edward J. Young, *The Book Of Isaiah* (Grand Rapids: William B. Eerdmans, 1972), 3:61.

11 Job 6:2-13, 7:1-7, 9:11-17, 25-33, 10:18-22, 23:1-9.

12 Habakkuk 1:2-3, 12-13b.

13 Matthew 27:46.

14 http://www.squidoo.com/seattle-rain (accessed July 2010).

15 http://www.islandnet.com/~see/weather/almanac/ arc2001/alm01nov.htm (accessed July 2010).
16 Hebrews 12:5, 8.
17 Psalm 56:8; Matthew 10:30; Psalm 139:16; Matthew 10:29.
18 Ray Besson and Ranelda M. Hunsicker, *The Hidden Price of Greatness*, cited by Jonathan G. Yandell, Garden Grove, CA from Leadership 16, no. 1, in PreachingToday.com.
19 Tan, *Encyclopedia of 7700 Illustrations*, 503.
20 Isaiah 59:1-2.
21 Romans 6:23; 1 John 1:7-10.
22 Matthew 4:1, 10, 16:23; Luke 22:31; Acts 13:10, 26:18; 1 Peter 5:8; Revelation 12:9, 20:10.
23 2 Corinthians 10:3-5, 12:7; Ephesians 6:12.
24 Matthew 17:22-23, 26:74-75; Luke 22:31-32.
25 John Piper, *When the Darkness Will Not Lift: Doing What We Can While We Wait for God and Joy* (Wheaton, IL: Crossway Books, 2006), 12, 23.
26 Ibid., 12. For additional reading, please note the helpful bibliography of resources Piper includes with his book.
27 Psalm 139:9-12a, 17-18.
28 Oswald Chambers, *My Utmost For His Highest* (Grand Rapids: Discovery House, 1963), 156, 167.
29 Foster, *Celebration of Discipline*, 84-95.
30 Chambers, *My Utmost For His Highest*, 293.
31 Nancy Gibbs, "And on the Seventh Day We Rested?" *Time*, August 2, 2004 in PreachingToday.com.
32 Sir Paul Reeves in a prayer at the WCC Seventh Assembly in Canberra, Australia, February 1991, in *Christianity Today* 35, no. 11 (October 7, 1991): 30.

Chapter Eleven
1 Ecclesiastes 3:1.
2 H. Norman Wright, *Seasons of a Marriage* (Ventura, CA: Regal Books, 1983), 4.
3 Daniel Levinson, *The Seasons of a Man's Life* (New York: Ballantine Books, 1978), 6-7, quoted in Wright, *Seasons of a Marriage*, 4-5.
4 Gary D. Chapman, *The Four Seasons Of Marriage* (Wheaton, IL: Tyndale House, 2005), bk.
5 David Roper, *Teach Us to Number Our Days* (Grand Rapids: Discovery House, 2008), 214, © 2008 by David Roper, and used by permission of Discovery House Publishers, Grand Rapids, MI 49501. All rights reserved.
6 Willa Cather, *O Pioneers!*, ed. Susan J. Rosowski, Charles W. Mignon, and Kathleen Danker (Lincoln: University of Nebraska Press, 1992), Introduction.
7 1 Timothy 6:17.
8 Wright, *Seasons of a Marriage*, 32-53.
9 MacDonald, *Ordering Your Private World*, 28-61.
10 I would highly recommend these two books: *Ordering Your Private World* by Gordon MacDonald and *Liberating Ministry from the Success Syndrome* by Kent and Barbara Hughes. In addition, please note the following books that might be helpful in dealing with the issue of drivenness and burnout: Robert Hemfelt, Frank B. Minirth, and Paul D. Meier, *We Are Driven: The Compulsive Behaviors America Applauds* (Nashville: Thomas Nelson, 1991), bk.; Frank B. Minirth et al., *How to Beat Burnout* (Chicago: Moody Press, 1986), bk.; and Richard A. Swenson, Margin: *Restoring*

Emotional, Physical, Financial, and Time Reserves to Overloaded Lives (Colorado Springs, CO: NavPress, 1992), bk.
11 James Dobson, *Straight Talk to Men and Their Wives* (Waco: Word Press, 1980), 136-137.
12 Wright, Seasons of a Marriage, 56.
13 Author unknown.
14 2 Samuel 11.
15 J. Robert Clinton, *The Mentor Handbook* (Altadena, CA: Barnabas, 1991), 17-1.
16 1 Corinthians 9:24-27; Philippians 3:8-10.
17 These percentages and general estimates were taken from The CIA World FactBook at https://www.cia.gov/library/publications/the-world-factbook/ (accessed July 2010).
18 National Center for Health Statistics, United States, 2008 With Chartbook, Hyattsville, MD: 2009 at http://www.cdc.gov/nchs/data/hus/hus08. pdf#026, Table 26, pp. 9, 20, 203 (accessed July 2010).
19 Proverbs 16:31, 20:29.
20 Revelation 21:1-5; 1 Corinthians 15:50-58.
21 2 Corinthians 4:16-5:8.
22 I would highly recommend reading the following book: David Roper, *Teach Us to Number Our Days* (Grand Rapids: Discovery House, 2008), © 2008 by David Roper, and used by permission of Discovery House Publishers, Grand Rapids, MI 49501. All rights reserved. It is a book about cultivating God's perspective on growing older. His musings and insights are profound and helpful.
23 Roper, *Teach Us to Number Our Days*, 159-160, © 2008 by David Roper, and used by permission of Discovery House Publishers, Grand Rapids, MI 49501. All rights reserved.

Chapter Twelve
1 Thoughts On The Business Of Life, *Forbes*, March 4, 1991, 160.
2 Craig Brian Larson, ed., *Contemporary Illustrations for Preachers, Teachers, & Writers* (Grand Rapids: Baker Books, 1996), 283.
3 Jayne Clark, "Sooner or Latte, He'll Get There," USAToday.com, October 13, 2005, submitted by Sam O'Neil, St. Charles, IL in PreachingToday.com.
4 Numbers 12:8; Exodus 33:11.
5 Exodus 33:18-23.
6 Stephen Charnock and William Symington, *The Existence and Attributes of God* (Grand Rapids: Baker Book House, 1996), 1:283-284.
7 Hebrews 13:8; see also Job 8:9 by way of contrast.
8 Read the Gospel of John, chapters 1 and 3.
9 Ronald Blum, "Yankees owner George Steinbrenner dies at 80," Associated Press, July 13, 2010.
10 R. Dwight Hill, "Honoring Gene Warr — A life That Is Counting For Eternity," *The Facts of the Matter*, September 21, 2005 at http://www.factsofthematter.org (accessed July 2010).
11 Roper, *Teach Us to Number Our Days*, 117, © 2008 by David Roper, and used by permission of Discovery House Publishers, Grand Rapids, MI 49501. All rights reserved.
12 Theodore W. Brennan, *I Looked* (Independence, MO: Gospel Tract Society, 1970).